The Thirteen -

Gentlemen in Exile

The continuing story of George Ransley and the Aldington Gang

Lyn Watts

The Thirteen -
Gentlemen in Exile

First Published September 2019

10 9 8 7 6 5 4 3 2 1

ISBN 978-1-9161518-1-9

Printed by Print Domain, 107 High Street, Thurnscoe, Rotherham, South Yorks S63 0QZ

Published by WattKnott Publishing, Testers, Whatlington, Battle, TN33 0NS England

For Mark

There is nothing more powerful than when two souls meet and understand each other's struggles and pain. When it's time for souls to meet, there is nothing on earth that can prevent them meeting, no matter where they are located!

Acknowledgements

With grateful thanks to Mark Ransley and Tony Hale for the idea; to Dennis Ransley and Sue Rodaughan for the information on their family trees. To Bruce and Paul Ransley and Megan Buchan for their guided tour of New Norfolk churchyards. To my readers of 'Gentleman in Blue' for their encouragement and the request for the follow-up book. Thanks also to Charlie Watts for his patience and proof reading, but most of all thanks to horses Jurgen and Murphy for their cuddles and rides when I was stressed and to Mac for being my borrowed cuddle dog in Tasmania!

Contents

Foreword

I originally spent two years researching George Ransley and the Aldington Gang - early nineteenth century Kentish smugglers - before I wrote Gentlemen in Blue. The book was very successful and had three reprints in its first year, putting it on its fourth printing. I, however, was bereft after finishing it. I had lived with George Ransley in my head for two years. I got to know him well, and the locations haunted by the gang also, and I was loath to leave them. To my delight I found Mark and Bruce Ransley on social media and their cousin Sylvana. We all became friends and I visited Tasmania in November 2018. I was welcomed as an honorary family member and enjoyed both the company of the Ransleys and Tasmania itself. Many of my readers had requested a sequel to the original book; this was also suggested in Tasmania by Mark and friend of the family, Tony Hale. I started this particular book a little half-heartedly - not really knowing what, if, or how much I would be able to find out. I surprised myself. I discovered that the information is still there - lots of it. It just needed ferreting out!

Whilst it reads like a novel at times, it is all based on true historical fact. Some conversations, inevitably, are down to poetic licence.

In my research, I found a link between an old friend of mine in the UK, Nadine Whitling, and James Hogben. She is a descendant on her father's side. I had already met a young man, Daryl Quested, who descends from Cephas and James. Karen, landlady of the Walnut Tree Inn, introduced me to Sue Rodaughan and her brother, David, from Victoria, Australia, when she was visiting the UK. She is related to both Thomas Gilham and John Bailey. Lots of information was provided by them both over a long afternoon tea!

Bruce Ransley introduced me to Dennis Ransley who, most generously, hosted an excellent lunch in the much respected Tasmania club during my stay in Hobart. I have now finished this book and there is little more to be discovered of the lives of my Kentish smugglers. I feel very saddened to leave them, but I now have lifelong friends in their descendants and am happily visiting Tasmania again this year (2019) by the kind invitation of Mark Ransley and Tony and Viv Hale. I may have lost my nineteenth century smugglers to history once more, but I have gained something of much more value. I have gained true and lifelong friends!

Lyn Watts, Battle, East Sussex May 2019

Condemned

Vile deeds, like poison weeds

Bloom well in prison air

It is only what is good in man

That wastes and withers there

(Oscar Wilde)

George sat in his cell thinking. It was Thursday, and his execution date was set for the coming Monday - 5th February! He knew that the Solicitor General had promised to intervene on behalf of himself and his fellow gang members. The hope was that their sentence would be commuted to one of transportation, but this was leaving it late. He hadn't had confirmation of anything yet. Would Knatchbull go back on his word? George was a courageous man, but he was getting worried. He didn't want to hang! What would become of Bet, his wife, and what fate would befall his children? His eldest son, George, was too young, at sixteen, to care for them all.

Sir Edward Knatchbull was their only hope. He was the local MP for Kent and a barrister at Lincolns Inn, London - he would later become Paymaster General, but that was in the future. A future he would enjoy if he could rely on the discretion and silence of George.

George had enough information and knowledge to ruin him - indeed, Knatchbull himself and several others in high stations - but he had enjoyed a good life thanks to Squire Knatchbull. He had built his house, The Bourne Tap, and chosen the location himself. It was out of the way, lying as it did next to open common wasteland. It was most convenient for both Ashford, Maidstone, and the runs to the coast and, often, to France.

Money had never been a problem during the last ten or so years. He had relished the life of a gentleman. He had quit his work as a carter at Court Lodge Farm in order to run the Aldington Gang of free traders - some would say smugglers - along with his wife's father (at first) and then her brothers, Samuel and Robert, with their uncle John.

George had the charisma to transcend all classes and a good business head upon his shoulders. He was popular and caring towards his fellow man. These qualities made him a fine and successful leader. Knatchbull had noticed these qualities and they had proved to be of mutual benefit to both of them. Besides which they genuinely liked each other and, in different social circumstances, they would likely have been close friends.

Now by the greed and treachery of some former gang members, alongside a run of bad luck, George and thirteen others found themselves languishing in Maidstone gaol under sentence of death. They were entirely dependent upon the wiles of their solicitor, Mr Platt, and the reliability of Sir Edward Knatchbull to keep his word and get their sentences commuted.

Knatchbull was a kind man; intelligent, generous and popular. He possessed the same qualities as George - albeit they came from very different backgrounds. This was the reason they had got along so well and had enjoyed the good working relationship they had had. Yes, George was sure he would keep his word. He was just cutting it a bit fine!

Then there was Sir Edward's cousin, Juliet. Oh how George had loved her! A young widow, they had enjoyed a passionate relationship; but he was no good to her now, wherever he was destined to end his days. No, his cousin, John, clearly admired her; he was a better man for her than he himself had been and would doubtless look after her in the future. That, at least, had set George's mind at rest.

He remembered that frosty night in October when they had been taken. It was just before 3am. Mattie, his eldest, just seventeen years old, had heard the door being broken down and had screamed out the code word to notify the household that the law was upon them. George had leapt up, pulled on his breeches and was still buttoning up his flies when Lieutenant Hellard and his men had burst into the bedroom. Wrapped in a sheet and screaming profanities, Bet was being restrained by one of the soldiers before she could smash the chamber pot over Hellard's head, while Mattie wailed at the discovery of their two dogs slain outside. George went quietly. There was little point in resistance. He had known that this would happen one day and now he had to rely on the skills of his solicitor, Platt, and the promises of Sir Edward Knatchbull, in his fight for life.

Handcuffed to the biggest dragoon, he was marched to join the others rounded up that night. They were his brothers-in-law, Samuel and Robert Bailey (Bet's brothers) Charles Giles, the local shoemaker, Thomas Denard, who lived on his own land at Aldington Frith, near George, where he kept horses. Also taken were Thomas Gilham (Dutchy due to his alias of Datchet Grey) and brothers Richard and William Wire. They were marched the seven cold miles to Fort

Moncrief at Hythe. George remembered with some amusement Juliet thundering up behind them when they reached Lympne - her hair streaming behind her, her horses' breath steaming in the frosty early morning and Juliet's wrath at Hellard causing him great discomfiture!

He had hoped that that was the end of it, but on a wet, stormy, November night ten of the others were taken. Two of them had turned King's evidence and two of them had been acquitted; that left fourteen of them in Maidstone gaol under sentence of death, awaiting the mercy of his majesty!

It was 6pm and George could hear the sound of locks opening and closing as the disgusting oatmeal porridge and half pint of milk, which constituted supper, was being served to the prisoners. This was the last meal until breakfast at 7am and, therefore, foul as it was, George would have to eat it since there was no alternative. He was lucky. He could afford to have better fare sent in from outside to supplement, the boring, barely adequate and rather tasteless prison diet from time to time. This diet was mainly of oatmeal porridge twice a day with bone meal broth or vegetable soup, sometimes containing boiled ox head served with bread for dinner at 1pm. A hard cheese with bread twice a week replaced the porridge supper. This 'haute cuisine' kept them alive and broke the boredom of their solitary existence in the newly reformed prison. In Maidstone each prisoner had their own cell containing a bucket with a lid, a pail of water, a wooden stool and a narrow, hard bed with a single blanket and an extremely firm pillow. Men under sentence of death were not expected to undertake any hard labour.

After the tasteless, lukewarm, supper George had plenty of time to think before lights-out at 9pm. Other prisoners attended lessons and learnt to read, write, or take on a skill such as carving. Such things were deemed pointless for those on 'death row' and George could read and write well enough anyway. He had always had a problem with figures, though, so George, his son, had kept all his accounts for him during his 'free trading' activities.

The free trade, George reflected; it had been almost inevitable that he would become involved in such a thing. He thought back over his life - forty four years of life - which, if his legal team didn't get a move on, might very well end on the Monday next at the end of a hempen rope!

He had been born on the 13th day of February in 1785 in Ruckinge, in the parish of Kenardington, near Ashford in the county of Kent. His Father was also George Ransley and his mother was called Hannah. His older cousins, William and James Ransley, had been the terror of the area. They had lived on the opposite side of the road to George's parent's cottage until their father wanted more seclusion and space. They then moved to a bigger and more gloomy-looking grey house in Kingsford Road in the village of Mersham, some four miles distant. It was situated in a remote area with the nearest neighbour being the parish workhouse. The whole Ransley family were involved in dark trades and the cousins ended their lives swinging from ropes on Penenden Heath, when George was just eighteen years old.

They had been hung for robbery - the theft of a horse - but they had also been involved in extortion, highway robbery and blackmail. Their father was involved in the 'free trade', as was George's own father. George remembered hushed voices and being banished from the family sitting room when his father was entertaining his 'friends'. Occasionally there had been raised voices and the sounds of fighting.

Once, when George was just a toddler, a body had been found in the pond of his father's field. It was never identified. The deceased had met with a very violent end. It had been a man aged about thirty years. He had had long black loose hair and was of a swarthy complexion. His hands had been tied. He also had a small grindstone affixed to his head with a larger one tied to his legs. This had rendered it impossible to reach a verdict of accidental death! His skull had been fractured - as were his nose and upper jaw. It was thought that the body had been in the water for about three weeks. No one was ever brought to trial for his death. The victim was believed to have been a smuggler from the upper part of the county and, although never formally identified, the rumour abounded that he was one Robert Eling from Biddenden.

In 1790 a small school was started in the lady chapel of St Martin's church, Aldington. When he was old enough to walk the four miles there, George had attended lessons with Mr W. Holmes, the teacher; albeit sporadically. He would learn just enough to read and write sufficiently, but was better employed helping his father in his various dealings.

When he was twelve George was employed by the farmer at Court Lodge Farm, which was a short walk from his home. He started as a general farm-hand, but soon his affinity with horses became apparent and he was employed as a carter/ploughman.

He became a valued employee, proving to   be   an expert horseman. He fell foul on one occasion when he was caught by the farmer stealing corn. He claimed it was to feed the horses and the farmer had no desire to lose such a good worker so he was forgiven. No one locally wanted to fall foul of the Ransley family.

When he was twenty three he met Elizabeth Bailey. The Baileys were a local family and famous for smuggling. They lived at Mersham. The whole family were involved and Elizabeth's father, Samuel, was the leader of a very successful band of men involved in the trade. He became known as Thresher Bailey since he had a habit of carrying a threshing flail to use on the heads of any pursuing excise men should the need arise. His half-brother, John, and his sons, Samuel and Robert, were also very heavily involved with the gang. Most of them lived in the villages and hamlets around Aldington, indeed the Walnut Tree Inn in that village had been their meeting point and headquarters. To blend into the night the gang wore dark blue gaberdines - these were long smocks -and this earnt them the name locally of the 'Aldington Blues'

By the middle of January 1809, it was apparent that Elizabeth was pregnant. A big buxom girl, she loved to party to excess and to play hard. She was a little younger than George, but had a wealth more life experience. The naïve, innocuous, George - as yet inexperienced in the wiles of women - was easily seduced by her worldly wisdom. The Baileys were delighted to have a Ransley joining the family (albeit by no choice of his own!) With an average height of six feet, the Bailey men were considered huge at a time when the average height for a male was five feet and six inches. They were also known to be as tough as old boot leather and not to be crossed under any circumstance.

So it was that on the 14th of February in the charming little church of St Rumwold's, at Bonnington, the twenty-four year old George stood, nervous and hot, under his starched stock, awaiting the Reverend Bridges who was to marry Elizabeth and himself. The ceremony was held under the watchful eyes of the male Baileys, both senior and junior, while Elizabeth would do her best to conceal the growing bump under her aprons.

Their marriage was a reasonably happy one despite their different temperaments. Elizabeth (Bet) was loud, brash and fiery, whilst George was quiet and reflective with a fastidious nature. Yet, he could be ruthless if the situation demanded it. Charismatic and caring, he had a good business head and could keep calm under pressure. They lived in a rented cottage in Bonnington a mile or so away from Aldington village, and George continued to work at Court Lodge Farm. George grew to love Bet since she was a strong caring woman and she proved to be a good mother.

Their eldest child, Matilda Blanche, was born on the 16th of July in 1809, followed in early February 1811 by a son, George. There followed another son, John, the following year. The family increased thick and fast after that, with a child born roughly every two years. Ann was born in September 1815 and died in the November aged just five weeks. Then she bore William in 1816, Robert in 1818, James in 1820, Anne in 1822, Edward, in 1823 and Hannah in 1825. Bet now found herself pregnant again. With his ever growing family George had needed to earn more than the low wages of an agricultural worker. Thresher Bailey was able to recruit up to a hundred men at any one time to help to unload and distribute the contraband smuggled over from France. It was landed on the beaches across the marshes. George was soon recruited and proved to be a valuable asset and a natural commander of men.

The earnings from one night's smuggling could be as much as a whole week's wage from the farm. Bailey senior soon grew to rely on George's quick brain, and cunning.

Many of the men recruited were local farm hands or small farmers. The blacksmith from Mersham joined them, as did men from Burmarsh and as far away as Hythe and Folkestone. The main gang consisted of twenty or so batsmen and tub men. The batsmen formed a circle around the tub men facing outwards and holding long heavy oak cudgels to beat off the government revenue men if the necessity arose. The tub men worked like lightning to cut the brandy barrels free from each other when they were all roped together on the beaches.

The tubs were then carried away, two to a man, strapped over their shoulders, or strung across the back of any ponies or horses they could muster. Most of the men bore scars to their hands and wrists from the occasional slip-up with their sharp knives in the dark whilst working so fast. George himself usually drove his favourite mare harnessed to his cart to take some of the cargo.

He thought of his poor mare. She had been such a good horse. He missed her. He supposed that she would stay with young George now, or go to his cousin George, who was churchwarden at St George's Church, Ivychurch. He had been useful to the gang in the past since they often used the crypt of the church to store their ill-gotten goods.

Buying boats cheaply from France meant that if they were spotted by the coastguard they could sink the cargo – everything was roped together - mark it with a floating gull's feather (attached of course) and scupper the boat. They were cheap enough to replace and there could be as much as 600% profit from a night's work.

George became the chief negotiator with the customers who bought the goods. There was little that local squire, Sir Edward Knatchbull, didn't either have a hand in or, at the very least, be aware of. He liked George. His charm and wit appealed to Sir Edward and he was pleased to be able to replenish his wine cellar and make a little extra income from the gang. A deal had been struck that meant more cash to buy uncustomed goods in France.

George gave up his job on the farm and his large family moved into a white house just outside Aldington village at Aldington Frith. This was an area of open common land away from prying eyes and conveniently placed for transporting the goods. George had built it himself to his own specification. It had a cart barn and stabling. There was all the grazing his horses needed on the common.

He explained away his sudden wealth by claiming to have found a stash of spirits whilst ploughing - the sale of which funded the building of The Bourne Tap, as he called the property. Of course the local gang members and the Baileys would never have allowed him to sell any contraband they had buried, but it had been a good cover, he thought to himself.

The free trade proved to be so lucrative that George employed the gang's own doctor. Ralph Hougham, from Brookland, would patch up any injured men. He had come to George with just the shirt on his back. His practice was not doing well and he had an ever growing family. He had to borrow a shirt to wear on laundry days while his was being washed. George had drastically improved his fortunes and, in return, he was the master of discretion in matters of the gang and their activities. Mr Platt, a highly respected solicitor, was also employed to fight any legal case brought against any gang member. Platt was paid handsomely by George, but he was good; very good! There was also a fund to care for the families of any members of the gang who were injured in their line of work with the trade!

By 1821 George and Bet had six surviving children, having already lost Ann at just a few weeks old.

The Walnut Tree Inn at Aldington became a resting place for the gang's goods and the landlord benefitted from this lucrative arrangement. The gang made the inn their headquarters and it was there that they held meetings at which they would plan their next run. It was ideally placed for signalling across the marshes to the boats waiting to come ashore. The tiny top room had a window high up and any signal would be directly visible across the pitch dark marsh. This became their main meeting room, and was only accessible through a steep ladder staircase.

Bet, being a party girl, opened the Bourne Tap to custom most Friday and Saturday nights. It became a 'blind pig' for selling back some of the smuggled liquor to the local gang members and travellers from afar. Noisy, smoky and raucous, these evenings held no appeal for George and he preferred to sit outside on his favourite mare, or else in the cart barn, planning his next run.

Thresher Bailey became more and more reliant on George and took a more minor role himself in the organisation of the gang's affairs

One of the local men who lived in the Frith Road was Cephas Quested. He knew the marshes better than most and would often lead a run back across the marsh. With a growing family to feed, Cephas was desperate for money; his main problem, though, was drink. He would tap the very tubs on his back when the mood was upon him. This proved to be his downfall.

A big, blustering man, he once got blind drunk in a field with his brother in law - a man called Gardener - on a freezing January night. They fell asleep. In the morning Gardener was dead. He had frozen to death. When he realised this Cephas exclaimed: "Ah well, he died of what he loved!"

On the 11th of February 1821 the gang had run a cargo into Camber. They were spotted on the beach by the blockade sentries who fired several warning shots to the patrols in the vicinity. They were pursued inland by the blockaders, led by young Midshipman McKenzie, who caught up with them at Brookland, on the Walland Marsh. A huge and bloody battle ensued with volley after volley fired into the smuggler's ranks and many a cutlass charge made. At the end McKenzie lay dead, shot in the chest, and two blockade officers plus six of their men were wounded.

The gang lost four dead and had sixteen wounded. After the fighting was over a very drunken Cephas was found flat on his back in a reed bed, fast asleep. On being woken, he had handed the man who had wakened him his pistol and told him to: "Blow a bloody officer's brains out!"

Unfortunately for Cephas that man was a revenue officer! Cephas had mistaken his blue jacket for one of the gang's blue smocks. Cephas was tried at Newgate and sentenced to death. George intervened and persuaded Squire Knatchbull to get his sentenced commuted to just death by hanging instead of 'hanging in chains'. That meant that his wife, Martha, could bring his body home to Aldington for burial in an unmarked grave in the churchyard of St Martin's, after his execution.

Cephas let the authorities believe that he was the leader of the Aldington gang. He refused to name any of the others. It was the most decent thing he had done in his whole life. In return George looked after his wife, Martha, and his children, until she remarried two years after Cephas' death. On every run, Cephas' share was dutifully given to his family and George frequently checked that they wanted for nothing.

Thresher Bailey retired from active service with the gang after this. The Battle of Brookland, as it became known, was a minor setback for the gang. They kept a lower profile for a while, but, with George as their new leader, plenty of activity was going on surreptitiously!

George heard the prison guards coming to check that lights were out. 9pm. Time for sleep. Not that sleep ever came easily in here. There was a narrow, hard, bed with a wooden pillow, then there was always shouting and noise from the other prisoners, not to mention the thoughts in his own head. What if the Solicitor General had let them down? He was meant to recommend his Majesty's mercy on them and spare them all the rope. The execution was set for Monday the 5th of February; this was Thursday night (the 1st), there was no news, as yet, on a reprieve. What of their families - The ones left behind in Aldington and surrounding villages?

George thought of all of his fellow gang members languishing at his Majesty's pleasure. Who would they leave behind at home? James Wilson, a twenty nine year old farmer with just his widowed mother; how would she cope without his income? George's own brother-in-law, Richard Higgins, married to Bets sister, Rhoda; she and their two children would be left behind in Bilsington. Bet's brother, Samuel, and uncle John from Mersham, were also with him.

John's wife Catherine - they had six children and Samuel's wife Sarah and their daughter would be cared for by the large Bailey clan, but without the supplementary income from the trade, money would be very tight. It had been Sarah Bailey's, Nephew, Edward Pantry, who had turned Kings Evidence and helped to convict the gang. Sarah had been a Pantry before her marriage to Samuel. That caused some friction in their marriage.

Then there was Thomas Denard, cousin of the Baileys; he left his parents and their small farm. Would they manage without him? Thomas Gilham, (Dutchy), brother-in-law to John Bailey, he and Frances, his wife, had numerous small mouths to feed. Charles Giles, the local shoemaker; his wife, Mary, and their three daughters would most likely end up living off the parish in the workhouse - a tragedy! Paul Pierce, the landlord's son from the Blue Anchor left behind Sarah, his missus, and their seven children at Bonnington. They would never manage without his income as a gardener. James Hogben from Ruckinge, also a gardener, had a wife and seven children. James Quested, related to the hapless Cephas, left a wife and seven children to feed at Hawkinge.

Then there were the young unmarried tearaways! Richard and William Wire were just eighteen and twenty years respectively. They had left a widowed mother and a brother behind in Aldington to manage their small farm without them. George had tried to fill a fatherly role for them after their own father was killed - struck by lightning in his own field. Sadly they were impressionable young rips and were heavily influenced by the newcomer from the North Kent's, James Smeed. He came to them with his young half-brother, Thomas. James had escaped detection and no one gave him away. They had elderly parents at Hythe, so James alone took the rap. He had, however, been instrumental in their downfall and George should never have allowed him to carry a firearm. At just twenty one he had escaped across the marshes to Aldington when the North Kent smuggling gang had been 'smashed up'! That bunch of ruffians had been far more ruthless than George's men and four of their leaders had been hung. James impressed the Wire brothers with his gun;, indeed it had been Richard, (Dick) Wire who had fired the fatal shot that had landed them all here.

George had much sympathy for the widow of the poor young officer who had been shot on Dover beach. The problem had been that young hothead, Dick Wire. He had fired in the dark to scare the blockaders, but he couldn't see. The musket balls had hit Richard Morgan and proved fatal.

George, himself, had neither carried, nor approved of, guns and now he was living with the result of allowing those boys to carry them! Not that he could have stopped them. Flushed with success after a previous run they had become rowdy and full of themselves. They had charged through the Walnut Tree Inn, whooping with joy, stealing anything edible they could lay their hands on and terrorising the locals. That was not George's way. He had always kept the locals on his side. That was why the gang had been so successful over a great many years. Once the youngsters had become cocky, local sympathy drained and with it the reputation and success of the gang. And these cells were where they had ended up!

George dozed fitfully. This was how he spent his nights in here - too many thoughts crowding his mind, disturbing dreams and waking many times during the night!

Friday morning started as usual. There was the jangle of iron keys in the lock at 6am and "slops out!" shouted up and down the cell block as buckets were changed and fresh water brought in for the morning ablutions.

Breakfast was at 7am. Sometime after 8am George received a visit from Mr Platt, his solicitor. He was told that the Governor of the county gaol had received a letter the previous day from the Solicitor General. Platt read it. "His

Majesty has graciously seen fit to spare their lives, but they are to spend the remainder of their lives as criminal exiles in a distant, foreign land and nevermore set foot upon English soil!" Their death sentence had been commuted to transportation for life! Although he couldn't be sure, Platt believed that they would be sent to Van Diemen's Land.

George felt his knees go weak! He had heard rumours about this place. It was, he had been told, on the other side of the world! He might as well be dead, he thought! They said it was a vast wilderness with natives who were constantly trying to kill the white man. He had also been warned that there were snakes that would kill you in an instant and spiders as big as a man's fist that could kill you with one deadly bite (if the natives hadn't got to you first!)

It had to be said, however, that the man who had been boasting of this the previous year, in the Farriers Arms at Mersham, had survived out there for his seven year transportation sentence, and lived to return home to tell the tale! George had also heard that there were opportunities. If you behaved and kept your nose clean, you could, after a year or so, apply for your family to join you. After a few years they would grant you freedom and give you land to farm.

That was provided you could build your own house from wood!

Would Bet and the children join him though? She had been pretty mad with him for getting caught. With nine children to care for and another one due at any day, she wasn't in the most reasonable of moods and had refused to make the twenty five mile journey from Aldington to Maidstone to see him. It was probably not a good idea anyway in her advanced state of pregnancy, mused George!

George came out of his reverie and turned to Platt. "Let the others know, can you? And please tell Bet and the children what is happening."

The Hulks

It is a kindness that the mind can go where it wishes

(Publicus Ovidius Naso)

The routine in the gaol ground on its grim way for the next two days. On the Monday morning, the 5th, a crowd had started to gather at Penenden Heath very early. All were looking forward to a day out to witness the mass execution of the fourteen men from Aldington.

Unbeknown to them at this time, they were to be cheated of such a spectacle, for at 7.30am, the very second breakfast was finished, the men were taken from their cells. They were handcuffed, strongly ironed and chained together then they were placed into a van for their marathon journey.

George, James Wilson, Charles Giles, James Hogben, James Quested and the Wire bothers were to be taken to Portsmouth to the *Leviathan*.

John and Sam Bailey, Thomas Denard, Thomas Gilham, Dick Higgins, Paul Pierce and James Smeed were travelling to the *York* at Gosport."

The van was one of the hard bone-shakers. It was crude and basic - unsprung and with wooden bench seats. In cold conditions and with maximum discomfort, they drove relentlessly; only stopping to change horses, and for occasional refreshment. By keeping up the speed on the terrible roads, they had reached Hampshire by the following evening.

George, and the men bound for Portsmouth, were dropped off first, whist the Baileys and the others were taken on the few further miles to Gosport.

They smelt the ship as soon as they stepped off the van - the stench of stagnant bilge water, stale cooking and unwashed bodies crammed too tightly together. The *Leviathan* stood dark and menacing against the dusky sky.

She was a third rate 'seventy-four' - a type of two-decked sailing ship of the line which normally carried seventy-four guns. Built in 1790, she had fought at Trafalgar before being stripped of all her proud naval finery and being demoted to a prison hulk in 1816. Where once her sails had proudly flown, now the masts were used as washing props, her gun decks housing too many men tightly packed together in small wooden compartments each housing fifteen men.

The Kentish lads were marched onto the ship and mustered on the quarter-deck to be received by the captain. Their prison irons were removed and handed back to the gaol staff. These latter departed home with alarming haste! The men were then taken to the forecastle to strip and thoroughly bathe themselves, before being given a new set of clothes made of a coarse grey material including a broad brimmed hat and heavy nailed boots. The barber then cropped and shaved every one of them, creating a total metamorphosis in their appearance.

They were then ironed again and given a hammock, two blankets and a straw mattress. Thus laden they were marched down below decks where the little wooden compartments were enclosed by iron palisading with lamps hung at regular intervals. Jeers and roars of welcome were shouted from the men already residing there. Ironic laughter followed them as they were marched past the occupied compartments. Within minutes they were housed in their new quarters.

The other prisoners had just finished school when our Kentish lads arrived. They were too late for supper so they were quickly rounded up for evening prayers in the chapel. It was half past seven. By eight o' clock they were mustered one last time before bed. Lamps went out at nine and the hatches were battened down. In these early years men could roam the decks freely at night, swapping any illicit goods such as tobacco and alcohol amid much arguing and cussing. In the later years of the hulks the wards were locked up at night. Our men, weary from their journey and sick at heart, strung their hammocks, climbed in and tried to catch a few winks of sleep - as much as the strange noises, snores and cusses of the other prisoners would allow!

With only a fourteen inch width to lie on and the hammock offering little support, sleep was elusive for George and the others. Just as it seemed he was finally drifting off, George heard the cooks being woken. It was three in the morning. A couple of fitful, uncomfortable hours later, the rest of the men were called up. It was five o clock.

Hammocks were to be rolled and stored away, then the men were allowed to wash themselves in large water troughs with cold (and rather murky) water. Afterwards they dressed in their coarse uniforms. Breakfast consisted of dry bread, rough and tasteless barley broth and a pint of cocoa.

After breakfast all of the decks were thoroughly scrubbed and cleaned by the prisoners until they mustered for shore work at half past seven. At this muster George and the others had to pass along the quarter deck past the guards and officers with their hats off and heads up. This was so that their features and gait became familiar to the guards should they attempt an escape. This would be repeated every day for a fortnight for all new prisoners. Once this had been done, and the ship was in good order, the men were rowed ashore with officers and guards, to work in the dockyards for the day.

The work varied. George and some of the others were put to unload timber and ballast from ships. Others dredged channels, or moved heavy cables. All the time they were obliged to wear a heavy iron on one ankle. If they had attempted escape, both ankles would be ironed and the weight of the irons increased. George noticed that James Wilson was pale, sweating and coughing continuously. On one occasion he fell. George and James Hogben went to his aid only to be pushed aside and cursed at by the guards who hauled him to his feet and set him back working again.

At twelve-o'-clock work stopped and the convicts were rowed back to the hulk for dinner. This consisted of boiled ox cheek, pease pudding and large very hard biscuit. Each man was given a pint of rather sour beer with this. James Wilson was taken after dinner to work on lighter duties aboard ship. He was put to work repairing clothes and shoes while the others were taken back to shore at half past one to begin the afternoon work. George was told that on foggy days, and in really bad weather, the convicts stayed aboard the hulks and there was no shore work. They actually worked for two hours per day less than the free labourers and were allowed to converse with them. They were, however, routinely searched by the guards to ensure that they were not secreting about their persons anything which might later assist an escape attempt.

Work was finished at five-thirty for the men, who were then rowed back to the ship and allowed to wash before supper. Supper, served at six, was either meat or cheese, potatoes and bread, again with the sour beer or, sometimes, water to drink. School commenced at half past six and all were required to attend. This was followed by chapel at seven-thirty and a final muster at eight. Lights out came at nine o clock and, in that way, 'day one' was completed for our lads during their sojourn on the hulks.

After a day of back breaking labour in the dockyard, our men fell asleep quickly despite their uncomfortable beds. George could still hear James Wilson's hacking cough as he drifted off to sleep!

This proved to be the routine on board everyday with the exceptions of Saturday evenings and Sundays. On Saturday evenings all men were expected to wash thoroughly and shave before going down below. Sunday morning, after breakfast, all prisoners were mustered onto the main deck for inspection of their clothing and new clothing issued to those who needed it. Then Divine service was held by the Chaplain, which all were required to attend.

The surgeon made daily visits to the ship. On day two James Wilson was declared as only fit for light duties on board. George doubted he would be deemed fit enough to be accepted onto the transportation ship, should one sail soon.

This was a dark period for our Kentish lads, separated from family and friends, and yet still on England's soil. It would come as a relief when a transport ship arrived for them.

James Wilson grew thinner and weaker daily. On the Wednesday night – the 14th of February and George's eighteenth wedding anniversary - James was extremely poorly. George knew he would be highly unlikely to recover from his debilitating disease. Consumption was ravishing his body. George sat with him as he lay in his small hammock. He spoke to him of Aldington and the surrounding villages, conjuring up visions of comfort and home until, finally, his breathing laboured and he fell insensible.

In the early hours of Thursday the 15th his laboured, rattling, breath finally ceased. George gently closed his eyes and thought of the waste of life. He was twenty-nine years old and left a Mother alone in Aldington.

He would be rowed ashore the following day, by the other elderly and infirm convicts and would be buried unceremoniously in an unmarked grave under the watchful eye of an officer!

On Wednesday the 21st of February, George was called aside just after breakfast by the quartermaster who told him that Bet had safely delivered a baby girl on the previous Sunday, the 18th. She was called Elizabeth after her mother and both were doing well. As he hurried back to catch the boat to shore for his days labour George reflected. A girl - ten children now; four girls and six boys, but he couldn't expect Bet to make the arduous two day journey to Portsmouth with a new born baby, only to stand on the shore for a ten minute meeting with him should the officers allow it. No he wouldn't meet this child until his family were allowed to join him whenever and wherever that may be. He felt his throat tighten and was suddenly homesick! He missed his family more than ever, and his home which he would never again see! It was a very dark time indeed!

All at Sea

"No grumbling or growling was to be heard throughout the ship. No, not even an oath (though the ship in general was well furnished with them, as in most of His Majesty's service)"

(Botanist Joseph Banks Journal, *Endeavour*)

Life continued aboard in its wearisome, monotonous, way until the March, when they heard that the *Governor Ready* would be leaving Portsmouth in April, bound for Van Diemen's Land. They, and their fellow offenders from Kent currently on the York, would be on board if their health and behaviour allowed.

This came as a huge relief for George and the others. On the 26th of March the *Governor Ready* appeared on the horizon to drop anchor a little away from the shore at Portsmouth.

She was a five hundred and twelve ton merchant ship, built in Prince Edward Island just two years previously in 1825.

George had heard rumours that the Captain, Mr John Young, and the Surgeon, Superintendent Thomas Braidwood Wilson, were fair kind men. Indeed the surgeon was paid half a guinea extra, on top of his naval pay, for every healthy, live convict he landed safely. They looked across at her, gleaming in the setting sun. The sky was red and grey behind her in the early evening light, the air smelt spring-like and the gulls flying overhead were calling. For the first time in weeks, George felt quietly hopeful and a little excited.

By March the 29th all the legal indents (the orders of transfer) for each convict were in place. The ship had taken on all provisions needed and embarkation commenced. George spotted the boat from the *York* coming in from Gosport. He risked the watchful eye of the guards and waved to his brother in law Samuel Bailey, who was on board with the others from Kent. They would embark first.

On the 31st it was the turn of George and the others to be taken across to the ship and to board her.

Although almost two years old, the ship still smelt new. Everything on her was clean and in order. George became aware of how dirty he and his fellow prisoners were by comparison; for the smell of the old *Leviathan* still lingered about them.

Mustered on the forecastle deck, they were received by the Captain and then taken below to wait quietly in line for their turn in the baths. First of all each man must strip and be thoroughly bathed. Wearing nothing but a towel, they then waited their turn to be examined by the Surgeon Superintendent to determine their fitness for the voyage.

Once they had passed as fit, they were each issued with a fresh set of clothes consisting of a denim jacket and waistcoat, a shirt of coarse linen, canvas trousers, yarn stockings and a woollen cap. Once donned in these, our boys felt human again and ready to face the long journey.

The men soon found that conditions on board the *Governor Ready*, were infinitely better than those on the hulks. The daily ration for each man was ¾ lb of good biscuit, then beef with either port or plum pudding for dinner. Pease soup was served four times a week and a pot of gruel with either butter or sugar was produced for breakfast. They each had three quarts of water daily. They were allowed four gills of Spanish wine weekly and, after three weeks at sea, each man would receive an ounce of sugar and an ounce of lime juice every day to guard against scurvy.

On the *Governor Ready* each man had eighteen inches of sleeping space compared to the hulks and the Royal Navy who only provided fourteen inches for their men. The men were split into 'messes' of six where a captain and a cook were elected. George was pleased to be with his other

Kent lads from the hulk and he was elected 'captain' while Charles Giles was 'cook'!

Before they set sail six 'captains of the deck' were chosen from the captains, to be responsible to the Surgeon Superintendent and to ensure that his orders were carried out. The ship's captain had charge of the crew and the ship herself, but the Surgeon Superintendent was in overall charge of the prisoners.

George was selected as a 'captain of the deck' from the one hundred and ninety-one prisoners on board. He would get on very well with Mr Wilson, as he was an intelligent kind man much the same as George himself.

Thomas Braidwood Wilson had been born on the 29th of April 1792 in West Lothian, Scotland. He was appointed Surgeon by the Royal Navy in 1815 and had married Jane Thompson just a year previously in 1826. This was his fourth voyage on a convict ship to Australia - the previous one had been on board the *Mangles* to New South Wales in 1826. Like many Naval Surgeons, he had a great interest in plants. In 1822 he had been granted land on the Macquarie River in Van Diemen's Land and was responsible for the successful introduction of the working bee for the honey industry there (having brought a hive over with him on one of his trips).

He would stay with the *Governor Ready* until her final fateful trip in 1829 where she was wrecked on a coral reef near Murray's island and sank within minutes. Thomas Wilson survived the 900 mile journey to safety in open boats despite many hairs-breadth escapes from danger. He ultimately settled on a farm in New South Wales in 1836 - called Braidwood - with his wife and daughter until his wife's death in 1838. He himself died suddenly in 1843 aged just fifty-one. This was, however all in the future.

For now the men familiarised themselves with the mess deck, where they would sleep and the rules of conduct on board the ship.

Prisoners must conduct themselves in a respectful manner to all the officers and to obey any orders issued by the Surgeon through his deck captain.

The prisoners must behave in a decent manner at all times, especially in morning and evening prayers and at divine service.

Cursing and all foul language, fighting, shouting, quarrelling or selling or exchanging clothes are strictly forbidden.

Any person stealing or secreting away any item belonging to the ships stores will be severely punished.

Each mess shall have a Captain who is responsible for the good order and cleanliness of the mess and to ensure the men wash themselves every morning and no one is to sleep in their clothes. Members of each mess are to sit together at meal times and each man takes his turn to wash and clean the utensils after each meal.

Smoking or striking lights down below, or attempting to wash and dry clothes will not be allowed under any pretence whatsoever.

Prisoners are warned that if found congregating at the bottom of the ladder leading to the water closets, they will be punished. No more than one person at a time allowed in the water closet.

Captains of the mess must see that the beds are neatly rolled up by 6am each morning and handed through to the crew on the upper deck for storage.

If at any time a prisoner has reason to complain of treatment or provoking language by any ships company, he is not to retaliate but to report to the surgeon through the deck captain so that the complaint can be investigated.

The Surgeon Superintendent has to impress upon the minds of the prisoners that their future prosperity and happiness will depend on their good conduct on board and on their report to the Governor of the Colony on arrival.

- (*Rules and regulations: *Lincelles*, 1862)

Routine on board for the convicts was very quickly established. Boarding was complete and it just needed for the tide and winds to be fair for sailing. This happened on Tuesday the 3rd of April. Anchor was weighed and the *Governor Ready* set sail for pastures new.

Life was ordered, but more relaxed than life on the prison hulks had been. The daily routine was:

4.30am – Prisoner cooks admitted on deck

5.30am- Mess Captains on deck to fill wash tubs while prisoners take up their beds and hammocks and pass to the hands on the upper deck

6am- prisoners commence washing their persons under the supervision of the Mess Captain, one half of the men at a time, half an hour being allowed to each group for this purpose.

7.30am- down all prisoners while Ships Company commence scrubbing upper deck and water closets

8am- breakfast

8.30am- One man form each Mess admitted on deck for the purpose of washing up mess utensils

9am- All prisoners on deck where Surgeon Superintendent will attend surgery and one man from each mess takes it in turn to clean and scrape dry prison deck and berths.

9.30am- Prison inspected then all prisoners assembled on deck for prayers

10am- One half of the prisoners sent on deck for exercise while the other half attend school under the superintendence of the Religious Instructor and his monitors

11.30am – School to break up

12midday- Dinner

12.30pm- One man form each Mess admitted on deck for the purpose of washing up mess utensils

1.30pm- half the prisoners admitted on deck for exercise, the remainder to attend school

4pm- School breaks up, down all beds and hammocks

5pm –Supper

5.30pm - One man form each Mess admitted on deck for the purpose of washing up mess utensils

6.30pm- Prayers

8pm- Down all prisoners

9pm- Rounds and lights out

On Tuesdays- every man to be shaved, mess Captains to supervise this

Wednesdays and Thursdays- Men allowed on deck to wash their clothes, Half one day, half the next. Saturdays - there was no school, bottom boards to be washed and dried on deck

Sundays- Divine service at 11am

(*Daily Routine: Lincelles, 1862)

The winds were behind them, the weather was set fair and soon Portsmouth harbour, and the shores of old England receded into the distance and out of their sight forever. The men felt a pang of sorrow as the land disappeared below the horizon. Would they ever see their loved ones again? What lay before them in the new world? But life was busy. Prisoners had to produce a weekly newspaper on board as a sort of boredom breaker. They were encouraged to write and put on plays, to have sing-arounds and, with good behaviour, were able to take turns steering the ship (under the watchful eye of the crew and guardsmen). Knowing their good behaviour would determine their fate on arrival at the colony, all of our Kentish lads behaviour was listed in the report as 'good and orderly'!

On the 11th of April Samuel Bailey reported to Mr Wilson, the ships surgeon and was admitted to the small ships hospital in the aft of lower deck. He was diagnosed with erysipelas. George had suspected as much; 'St Anthony's fire' as it was colloquially known, was an infection of the skin; most probably picked up during his stay on the *York*. He developed a high fever, chills, shaking and a headache. George sent him, reluctantly, to the Surgeon, but, by then, he had nasty red skin lesions of raised blister-like spots and was vomiting. A few days of extra, high quality rations, Iodine washes on the lesions and he was fit enough to be discharged on 28th the April.

Apart from a few minor ailments, our Kentish lads enjoyed good health on the voyage. One man was to die on the journey. A stranger to our lads, he was buried at sea with minimal ceremony. Not a bad tally from one hundred and ninety-one men - unlike the notorious condition on the ships of the second fleet in 1790 when, from six ships, two hundred and seventy-two died on, or shortly after, the journey to Sydney Cove. Memories of that disaster were still fresh on the minds of the older men some thirty odd years later.

The weeks went by in the routine that was common on board transport ships at that time. Whilst the Chaplain tried to instil an atmosphere of morality and spirituality, yet there were still occurrences of gambling, petty theft and other forms of immorality!

The weather was set fair, winds were with them and they were making very good time. After about sixty days at sea they approached the equator. Rumours were spread on the ship that father Neptune himself, would visit the next morning to initiate the 'griffins' in crossing the equator. All novices, or griffins as they would then be known, were to assemble on the lower deck by 9am.

This only applied to crew members, and the 'griffins' (known as pollywogs by sailors from America) were men who had never before crossed the equator. If well behaved and orderly, the prisoners would also be allowed on deck to watch the initiation ceremony.

Thus it was that just before 9am the prisoners were assembled up on deck to watch the proceedings. A giant effigy of father Neptune was tied to the prow of the ship facing the deck and complete with trident. One by one the blindfolded griffins were led up by two of 'Neptune's Constables'. They were, in turn, strapped to a plank of wood, their faces lathered with a mixture of soap and paint then tilted head first into a large barrel of water and ducked three times. Needless to say, water and soap flew in every direction along with the general roars of the victims and the jeering laughter of some of the old hands.

By the end of this very entertaining ritual, everybody involved, including the captain himself, was soaked through. Even the prisoners had an unintended shower, as did the Surgeon Superintendent, but all took it in such a spirit of fun as had been intended, and all enjoyed the 'Crossing the Equator' ceremony. It was certainly a welcome break to their routine.

George and the others enjoyed a wealth of new experiences on the voyage. The weather and the daylight changed. The very sky and the smell of the air was different to anything they had known back home in Kent.

Day after day passed with nothing for a man to witness save mile after mile of ocean. Then, after about three months at sea, land was espied on the horizon. It was rumoured to be their destination.

Since the ship had crossed the equator the weather had been deteriorating. *The Governor Ready* pulled into harbour on the 31st of July 1827.

It was a cold day. There was blue sky and a thin covering of snow on the huge, dark, brooding mountain that seemed to dominate the small town of Hobart - where the ship sat at anchor. Despite this the beauty of the place was apparent to all of them. Crisp, but bright, the sky had a hue never before seen by these men. They had been used to the soft pastoral surroundings of a Kentish summer. Here was winter - even though it was the end of July. Everything seemed topsy- turvy to them. Despite the docking of the ship, routine on board would continue in exactly the same way until the Port Health Officer and the Principal Superintendent of Convicts had boarded the ship and were happy with the condition of all of the convicts on board. They were also there to receive any complaints from the prisoners regarding their treatment during the passage.

Both Captain Young, and Thomas Wilson had proved to be kind, good and fair minded men. The prisoners had no complaints at all. By 1827 conditions generally had improved greatly on the convict transport ships. Often they surpassed those on the free emigrant ships.

There would be another chance for the men to register any complaint once ashore since there would be an inspection by the Governor of the colony or his deputy. But for now the men had to wait on board for their paperwork to be put in order and then they would discover their fate -

where they would be put to work, for whom and in what capacity. They were told that this would take several days. The Surgeon Superintendent would have to report to the Governor of the colony with his journal and reports of every convict on board. This provided sole proof of that man's status as a transported convict; his identity, name and the name of the ship. This was, in turn, handed over to the Muster Master who constructed two volumes of information, each convict occupying a single line - one volume was to stay in the colony with the other to be returned to Great Britain. The Muster Master and the Principal Superintendent of Prisoners, would board the ship once the information had been gathered. Each man would be interviewed and minutely examined by them to determine his appearance, character, intelligence quota, work skills and capabilities. Once completed, the Governor's office would then find assignments for each man and they would be sent off to their new posts.

George had enjoyed a good relationship with Thomas Wilson, the surgeon. Whilst from very different social backgrounds, they were of equal intellect. George found him similar to Sir Edward Knatchbull. Thomas Wilson, in turn, had recognised the potential in George.

Following the death of the convict on board, George found Mr Wilson, looking glum, with his head in his hands. He sat with him and told him of James Wilson's death and how he had eased his passing. Thomas Wilson opened up to George about how hard he tried to deliver his charges, whole and hearty, to their destination. They spoke of their respective homes and spent an interesting hour together, convict and Surgeon Superintendent, sharing a pipe of tobacco; for once on the same level and in friendly harmony. George had carried out his duties as deck captain diligently and with efficiency. His conduct was noted as 'good and orderly' and he showed initiative. He would get a glowing report from the surgeon which would stand him in good stead for a future employer.

Word soon spread around the Governor's office in Hobart that the new consignment of men from Kent were a useful bunch with a wide knowledge of farming, horticulture and hop growing between them. Despite this, it was the 10th of August before the Kent contingent were assigned and ready to leave the ship.

Armed with their clothing allowance, they were sent off to their future employers. The annual clothing allowance per man was two woollen suits, three pairs of strong stock keeper's boots, four shirts and a hat. With this, and their written authority from the Governor, they left to face their new lives.

Pastures New

They tried to bury us

They didn't know we were seeds

(Mexican Proverb)

George was assigned to public works, looking after sheep and cattle on one of the biggest stock farms in the new land. It was situated by the Derwent River in New Norfolk. Food rations and working hours were better than those of some of the free settlers. With nowhere to escape to except the bush, George had as much freedom as he wished.

He was given knives and a gun - to shoot kangaroos. This would provide extra clothing and rations for him. He kept two dogs to help him to round up the sheep and had soon learnt to build his own shelter from leaves and turves when away from the main farmstead.

There were only two escape routes from the island and both would risk death. An escape into the bush was possible but the old trackers and army men were hunting the few remaining bushrangers by this time. If one were caught by the indigenous people they would kill you; so that was the first option more or less closed to all but the mad, the desperate or the foolhardy! The other route, by sea, would bring one up against the army. The end result would be to suffer under the harsh regime of a chain-gang; ironed and under the watchful eye, and, often, fearsome lash, of an officer all day.

George was very relieved with his situation. It could have turned out so much worse for him. He grew to love the land and the animals and soon found common ground with Mr Grey, his employer. In turn Mr Grey became more and more reliant on George and trusted his experience and judgement. In summer he was only required to work a forty-five hour week and far less in wintertime. He had spare time to help other local farmers for pay. He believed that, in time, he might be able to rent some land himself to start cultivating it. Rations were plentiful, with ten and a half pounds of meat and flour, seven ounces of sugar and two of salt weekly with a whole variety of fresh vegetables in season.

George decided to keep his head down and to work hard and well. He would be loyal to his employer. In that way, he might be able to bring Bet and the children over when the time was right. He had the right qualities – initiative, hardiness, courage, tenacity and adaptability. He soon learnt bush craft and how to hunt the ever useful kangaroo. At forty five years old, he stood five foot six and three quarter inches tall. He had blue eyes and brown hair. He was reliable, strong and good at quick decision making. He soon became indispensable to his employer.

Our men were to feel very much at home in a very short space of time. Rural areas, such as New Norfolk, where most were assigned, looked similar to Kent in landscape and the atmosphere was familiar to them. The weather was not dissimilar to the Kent climate either, although the summers were hotter.

Charles Giles, initially, was put to farming, but after just three months, he, like James Smeed, was assigned to the field police force. At first glance it seemed strange to put convicted criminals in positions where they were expected to catch others. They were furnished with pistols and trusted to escort other prisoners. However, it worked very well; for the need was for tough and resilient men to catch others similar to themselves. They were able to think like their prey and, for the most part, gain their respect fairly quickly. Charles didn't intend to stay in the police, and, upon gaining his freedom, he returned to his old trade of shoemaker.

Paul Pierce was initially assigned to the Colonial Secretary, John Burnett Esquire, possibly as his gardener. James Quested was assigned as a gentleman's servant, The Wire brothers, Thomas Denard, Thomas Gillham, Richard Higgins, James Hogben and the Bailey's were all, like George, assigned to farmers in various roles - ploughmen, carter, or general farming labourer.

Sad news had reached Paul Pierce shortly after his arrival in Van Diemen's Land. By the time that *the Governor Ready* had been halfway through its journey, his baby son Charles had died back in Kent. Within a few months of his arrival, news reached him that his daughter, Celia - known as 'Seeley' - had also died. It had happened just three days after the ship had docked in Hobart.

This must have affected Paul deeply. He was half a world away from his family and unable to comfort them. He coped with it in the best way he could find by seeking comfort where he could. On the 5th of February 1828, he was reported for 'indecent and immoral conduct with one Elizabeth Frankland in the service of his master.' Paul was reprimanded while poor Elizabeth was put into solitary confinement, on bread and water, in a cell in Richmond gaol for seven days!

Paul had married Sarah Deblaine around 1814. Within ten years they had produced seven children, three sons and four daughters. Paul worked as a gardener for Sir George Blessington at Bonnington; however, his parents owned the Blue Anchor at Ruckinge, so Paul became a master hop grafter. This was so important in producing the fine Kentish ale so popular with the locals. Hops had been grown in Tasmania from the early 1800's. From 1846 onwards New Norfolk also boasted some fine hop fields and oast houses. Paul would undoubtedly have been able to put his skill with hops to good use.

Paul was thirty five years old when he arrived in the colony. He stood at five feet four inches and had brown hair with grey eyes. He had scars and tattoos on his arms. About eighteen months after arriving, in late 1828, Paul applied for his wife and children to join him. His employer, Mr Burnett, had to certify that Paul had the means of supporting his family and that they would pose no expense to the government after their arrival. The application referred to

Sarah and children, George aged fourteen, Mary, Sarah, Dene, and right down to John aged two.

Governor Arthur approved the application on the 24th of November 1828, ignorant of the fact that Sarah and the Children had set sail on the *Harmony* a month before Paul had applied for them to join him! One cannot help but wonder what the consequences of a refusal might have been!

If they worked well and were orderly in conduct, the men could ask their employer's permission for their wives and children to join them from England. This could be anytime from a year into their sentence onwards. It was dependent upon the individual employer requesting permission from the Lieutenant Governor for the families to travel over and giving a good reference on the men's conduct, behaviour and industriousness. The employer also had to agree to enter into a bond for their maintenance and support upon their arrival in the colony. In reality most of the men were able to work for the neighbours of their employers in their spare time and make enough cash to support them themselves.

John Bailey was uncle to Samuel even though he was younger than him by some eight years. He stood a whopping six feet one inch, with brown hair and eyes, a large mole on his left arm and various scars on his hands plus two on his left cheek. Aged thirty four years on his arrival, he left his wife, Catherine, and six children at home in Mersham, Kent. He was assigned as a farm labourer.

Samuel Bailey, nephew to John, was forty four years old on arrival, five feet eleven inches and he too had brown hair and eyes. He was brother to George Ransley's wife, Elizabeth, and Richard Higgins' wife, Rhoda. Back in Kent he had been second in command to George and trained most of the gang members for their roles in the free trade. He was a competent sheep shearer and was assigned to Mr Edward Bisdee. Married to Sarah Pantry - it was her nephew, Edward, a former gang member, who had turned King's evidence and testified against the other gang members. The couple had a daughter, Ann. The fact that Sarah's nephew had been partly instrumental in the downfall of the gang caused some friction within the marriage. When he arrived it was unclear whether Sarah would ever join Samuel in the colony.

Thomas Gillham was, within a few months, assigned to William Lyttleton of Norfolk Plains. He wrote to the Colonial Secretary, in the April of 1828, requesting that the Lieutenant Governor give permission for Thomas' wife, Frances, and her six children to join him. He was advised to wait until he had been in the colony for a year and then would be encouraged to resubmit the request.

Thomas was born in April 1803 to Elizabeth Gilham, an unmarried mother from Aldington. His father was believed to be Thomas Carpenter. Thomas, himself, often went under the name of Thomas Carpenter. More commonly he had his alias of Datchet Grey and was known as 'Dutchy' by the other gang members. Thomas had worked long hours as a farm hand at Court Lodge Farm - as had many of the other gang members. Despite the fact that he often worked ten hour days, he still found time to court Frances Furner. Frances was a twenty seven year old unmarried mother of three children when Thomas married her. Frances was pregnant with their own child, Louisa, when they married in 1823 and Louisa was born just seven months later.

Thomas' behaviour on the hulk and *the Governor Ready* was described as 'orderly and correct'. Twenty four years old on his arrival in the colony, he was described as five feet seven and a half inches tall, with brown hair and hazel eyes. He had a scar on his arm and moles on his neck and shoulders. He was one of the inner circle of twenty or so batsmen (as were the rest of the convicted men). These had protected the tub men, whilst they were unloading the smuggled cargo, by forming a ring around them, facing outwards with big oak cudgels to stave off any pursuing revenue men.

Thomas was assigned to Joseph Archer at Lake River, along with Thomas Denard. Archer was building a beautiful country estate (Panshanger) which had extensive nurseries of oak, ash and elm trees, a flock of a thousand sheep and a large herd of beautiful mares and colts. The house had breath-taking panoramic views.

Archer was known to have a quick temper and had even been known to beat his convict servants. Thomas seems to have escaped his wrath, but was very soon reassigned to Archers' neighbour, Lieutenant William Lyttleton, who was building his estate, 'Hagley', near Westbury.

Thomas Denard was also assigned to Joseph Archer, but seems to have stayed on the Panshanger estate for longer than Thomas Gilham had. He too was aged twenty-four on his arrival and was five feet seven inches tall with brown hair and hazel eyes. Described on his record as a farmer/ploughman, he was soon reassigned - in 1830 - to Mr Andrew Gatenby who had fifteen hundred acres of land at Penyroyal creek which he called 'Barton'. He built a substantial flour mill there, which served the district for more than fifty years.

Thomas was unmarried and left his parents behind in Kent. He was a cousin, on his mother's side, to the Baileys - Samuel and Rhoda, Richard Higgins wife, and Elizabeth, George Ransley's wife, who had both been Baileys. John Bailey was his second cousin. Both his and their maternal grandmother was Mary Ransley. Given his ticket of leave in 1835, he met and married Ellen McCabe, a sixteen year old local girl, on the 9th of June 1838 - the same month he gained his conditional pardon. By then they were living in Brighton. The couple went on to have eight children; however, two of them died in infancy. In 1842 Thomas was declared bankrupt, having accumulated debts of £120. The young couple moved to Oatlands to be nearer to his cousins and he took employment as a stockman/agricultural labourer. He and John Bailey were charged with stealing a cart harness in 1845, and taken into custody. Thomas was charged with stealing the harness and John with receiving it. Thomas was eventually acquitted and John was discharged without trial through lack of evidence.

Shortly after this Thomas, Ellen and their children left the colony aboard the schooner *Lillias* and sailed for Port Phillip, in Victoria on mainland Australia. Here they had another daughter, Sarah, in 1852. Ellen became unwell following this child's birth. She developed a fever and gradually got worse. The Doctors diagnosed 'milk fever' - these days known as puerperal fever. Thomas watched helplessly as she worsened. He held her hand as she passed away. Baby Sarah seemed to have been the cause of her mothers' death and, in March 1852, Ellen was buried in St James Church at the age of just thirty. Thomas died on the 13th of November 1880 of 'general debility' at his home in Emerald Hill, Victoria. He had survived to the age of seventy six.

Richard Higgins was married to Rhoda Bailey, sister to George's wife Elizabeth. He was an agricultural labourer from Bonnington. When he was twenty three he had had a bastardy order taken out against him by Rhoda (once their son, Edward, had been born). Unfortunately Edward died in the January of 1819 aged just four months. Although they lived apart in the May of 1821 a daughter, Jane, was born to them and Rhoda made another bastardy order against Richard. They married three years later and another daughter, Mary Ann, was born to them. By the time he married, Richard had become a gamekeeper for a large local estate.

Upon his arrival in the colony, Richard was assigned to a local J.P., Samuel Hill Esq. He owned land near Campbell Town where he served as local magistrate and lived on his estate, Gadesden.

In April 1828 Richard forwarded a petition to the Governor requesting that his wife and daughters be allowed to join him.

James Hogben was originally from Folkestone in Kent. He had moved to Ruckinge where, upon his transportation, he had left his wife Ann (née Kember) and their seven children. Aged forty one when he arrived in the colony, his report from *the Governor Ready* described him as very orderly and correct. He was a gardener and was assigned to a Mr T. C. Simpson. He attempted an escape early on. He had been working in the garden one day and he needed some more poison for the slugs. He was entrusted to go into town to buy some with another convict, also in Mr Simpson's employ. They decided to stop by at the tavern in the town and too many ales were imbibed! Emboldened by the influence of alcohol, they decided to escape. Heading for the bush they spent the night sheltering as best they could. The alarm was raised when they failed to return to their employers. The constables were summoned and they had caught up with them by the following afternoon – wandering without purpose and hopelessly lost in the wilds of New Norfolk! They were returned to their employer but the episode meant that, as punishment, James could not apply for his family to join him as early as the other Kent men were able to.

His wife, Ann, did not join him until 1830, by which time he had been in the colony for three years. His three eldest children were settled in Kent with their lives established so it was only his four youngest children who travelled with their mother. They all embarked on the *Mellish* with Jane Seath, the wife of James Quested, and her children. He was assigned to his wife in 1833 and gained his ticket of leave in 1835. Given his conditional discharge in 1843, his family, by then, were living in a brick house in York Street, Launceston and they had another daughter (aged between one and seven in the 1842 census). His sons were listed in this document as being between the ages of twenty one and forty five years old. Theirs was always a stormy relationship. Ann and James spent some years apart. James left Launceston, with his son, on the 17th of April 1850 bound for Melbourne on the *Shamrock.*

Wife Ann died in Launceston in 1857. She had never really forgiven James for bringing them all to the impasse they had found themselves in. He himself died on the 22nd of May 1858 from 'decay of nature'. He was described as a gardener on his death certificate. His death was registered in Launceston, so he must have returned from Melbourne before the end.

James Quested was born in Swingfield, Kent, on the 22nd of April 1791. He was a cousin to James Hogben since their mothers were sisters, and he was thirty five years old upon his arrival in Van Diemen's Land. He had lived at Hawkinge with his wife Jane (née Seath), and their seven children, where he owned fourteen acres of land. He had been a sawyer and a gentlemen's servant in the service of Sir J. Bridges. Described on his convict record as being five feet seven and a quarter inches, he had brown hair and grey eyes.

On arrival he was assigned to Doctor Desailey as a gentlemen's servant. He stayed there until he was assigned to his wife in 1832. She had sailed on the *Mellish* arriving on the 22nd of September 1830. James had submitted his request for her to join him in the August of 1828 so it had taken over two years to accomplish. He gained his ticket of leave in 1833 and his conditional pardon on the 9th of March 1839. By this time he was living at 7, Melville Street, Hobart. He was still at that same address when he died on the 29th of October 1877. He was simply listed as a pensioner. Melville Street is just a few yards away from Harrington Street where Charles Giles had lived until his death in 1873. James' friend, James Page, and his son-in-law, John Rowlans, were appointed as executors of his will. He left instructions for them to sell his estate either by public auction or private sale, the proceeds to go to payment of his 'funeral and just debts' and to invest the rest in Government securities in Tasmania in the names of his said trustees - the interest and annual return from these to go to his widow, Jane. If she were to predecease him the said monies were to go to his children and to be kept in trust for any minors. If those children were already deceased, it reverted to any issue they may have produced.

William Wire was born in Aldington Kent in June 1808. He was aged just twenty when he arrived in the colony with his older brother, Richard. He was described as five feet seven inches tall with brown hair and hazel eyes. He had scars on his left fingers and wrist, most likely from rapidly cutting roped barrels of brandy in the dark during his days at the free trade. Both he and his brother, Richard, left a widowed mother and another brother in Aldington. Their father was already dead. He had been struck by lightning in one of his own fields. The boys had been farm hands back home so William was assigned to Mr G. Cartwright as a farm servant until 1832 when he was assigned to Mr J. O. Gage. He gained his ticket of leave in 1835 and conditional pardon on the 29th of May 1839.

There is no record of him marrying and he had no known issue. Always close to his brother, when he became unwell, Richard went to him and stayed by his side until the end. William had developed a skin infection in the late November of 1845. Despite the regular iodine washes and extra fresh food rations from his employer, the infection spread to his blood and he soon became delirious. Richard held his hand and they spoke of the good times on the beaches of South Kent and the marshlands. They reminisced about the night time runs and the drinking sessions in the Bourne tap back home. William died in Brighton, Tasmania, (about twenty three kilometres from New Norfolk) on the 30th of December, aged just thirty seven years with his loyal and heartbroken brother by his side. He was listed as a farmer and his cause of death is given as erysipelas.

Richard Wire was also born in Aldington but in August 1805. He was aged twenty two upon arrival and was described as five feet seven and a half inches with brown hair and grey eyes. He too had scars on his hands and two moles on his left arm. He had been assigned to John Sinclair as a farm hand and gained his ticket of leave in 1835. He was given a conditional pardon on the 15th of May in 1839 and seems to have become a farmer/ploughman in New Norfolk. As with his brother, there is no record of him marrying or having issue. He seems to have led a lonely and somewhat solitary life for the forty three years following the death of his brother. He was found dead in a New Norfolk street on the 4th of December 1888 aged eighty three. His death certificate described him as a pauper at the time of his death.

James Smeed. James and his brother Thomas had been members of the North Kent gang of smugglers back in England. When the gang was 'smashed up' - caught by the authorities - four of their leaders had been hanged. James and his brother, Thomas, had escaped across the marshes and fell in with the Aldington gang. It was believed that it was through the Smeed brothers that guns were first introduced to the Aldington gang. George himself never approved of, nor ever carried, firearms.

Thomas was not caught with the other gang members and no one gave him away. He and James had elderly, dependant, parents so James kept quiet and accepted his fate. It seems that Thomas had been doubly lucky in evading capture.

James was two years older than his brother, having been born in Hoath, near Herne Bay, Kent, in 1804. The North Kent smuggling gang operated in that area until their arrests in 1822. It was then that James and Thomas came across the marshes to the 'Blues'. They brought some of the more forceful practices, learnt from the north Kent's, with them.

He was a ploughman and groom at Mr John Brissenden's Bank House Farm in Aldington, where he had lived. Having been captured in the November raids, he was taken to the York Hulk and then on to *the Governor Ready*.

Aged twenty three on arrival, James was described as being five feet seven inches tall, with brown hair, grey eyes and high cheek bones. Rumour had it he was rather angelic looking and he had a scar on his left forefinger. James was drafted into the field police to replace a man who had been granted his ticket of leave. In 1826 Governor Arthur used the best behaved convicts in the police to pursue bush rangers and other runaway convicts. Later, once the bush rangers had been subdued, they dealt with attacks on the settlers and their property, by the Aboriginal people.

In July 1830, he was fined for drunkenness; then, a year later, in the July of 1831, he was escorting a former Government employee, turned forger, from Launceston to Hobart. He had found a kindred spirit and they got on a little too well. James chose to take him via the Clyde and New Norfolk route, stopping at the Bush Inn, rather than taking a quicker, more direct route. They enjoyed a drunken carousel for a few days, and eventually arrived (late) at their destination. These shenanigans earned him dismissal from the office of constable for 'gross disobedience of orders'!

In 1835 he was, once again, employed as a constable in the field police - his tough and fearless nature being invaluable to them. He was rewarded with a free pardon and reward money of sixty three pounds six shillings and eight pence for his role in apprehending the, at that time, famous bushrangers Jeffkins and Brown.

It was reported that James, along with three other constables - Smith, Buckley and Burbridge - were pursuing a man named Britton. They had run out of provisions and were returning from Port Sorell to the Tamar for supplies when they accidently came across the aforementioned bushrangers.

The Hobart Town Courier reports on the 6th of February 1835-

They accidentally met two miserable looking creatures, half emaciated, and in most wretched attire. They had worn-out moccasins on their feet, and the one had an old blanket wrapped around him, with holes for his arms, while the other was clothed with an old grey jacket, put on as trousers, the sleeves serving to cover the thighs. They were however, well-armed, and immediately bid the constables defiance. They proved to be Brown and Jeffkins: Smith stepped forward calling on them to surrender, when he received a shot in the breast from Brown which killed him on the spot. Jeffkins also fired and wounded Buckley severely in the arm, who notwithstanding returned the fire and mortally wounded his antagonist, while Smeed levelled at Jeffkins and shot him dead. Brown was then secured, and is now lodged in Launceston hospital.

A week later, the Courier's report from a member of the coronial jury provided further detail:

Jeffkins, after Brown fell, got behind a tree and fired at the constables, one of whom named Smeed took a circuit round and fired at Jeffkins, shooting him right through the head.

From 1836 James left the police force. He was working with a pioneering family called Henty. It seems that he was employed in the capacity of minder/bodyguard to their twenty five year old son, Stephen. He left Van Diemen's Land for Victoria with that family soon after leaving the police. Stephen Henty was an explorer, travelling to places the white man had never before ventured. He needed someone tough and resourceful to help and protect him. He and James travelled and met with many adventures together. They seemed to have a deep admiration and mutual understanding, and became very close. James took good care of his charge at a time when the indigenous people of the land were out to kill the white settlers. With his pretty boy looks and wiry, hard-as-steel nature, James got them through many a danger.

Having learnt how to use guns in his days in Kent and in the police force, James proved to be a good marksman against their Aboriginal opponents. This saved both their lives on more than one occasion.

One time, in the first few months following their arrival in Victoria, they were crossing some particularly wild bushland. Suddenly from nowhere a spear whizzed past Stephen's ear and buried itself in a tree trunk, missing him by millimetres. It had been thrown from a 'woomera' - a type of spear thrower invented by the same Aboriginal folk who had set upon them. Being a superb marksman, James managed to fire his gun and save their skins. He sent the tribal folk scuttling off in terror, but they needed to move on quickly before the natives returned with reinforcements.

Stephen Henty was both grateful and in awe of him, they looked into each other's eyes and recognised kindred spirits. A slow smile spread over Stephen's face and, despite the dangers, he knew he was happiest on his travels and adventures with James. They reached a special understanding and friendship that day, when finally they were safe enough to make camp for the night.

In 1837 they brought the first flocks of Merino sheep from Portland to the family runs at Muntham, Sandford and Merino Downs. James helped with the droving.

The Henty brothers, Stephen, Edward and John, first occupied Mount Gambier when James, in his role as stockman for Edward, saw the dim bluish outline of the mount from one of the hills near Casterton. He reported back to his employers. Edward Henty sent James and another man called Frost to investigate it. After a thorough investigation of the land, James pronounced it as 'good land and well worth occupying'. The family took it on under license from the New South Wales Government and John Henty brought over a large herd of cattle to graze it. James Smeed was, therefore accredited with being the first white man to reach Mount Gambia, later known as Moorak.

Whilst James worked as stockman, drover and minder for all three Henty brothers, it was his long, dangerous and frequent journeys to the plains with Stephen that he really relished. The two men were very close and enjoyed dodging the danger posed by the mysterious Aboriginal people. These latter were stealthy - good at suddenly appearing - and skilled with arms. James and Stephen had to be quick and alert to avoid being killed by them. James proved to be a better shot than them and employed ingenious tactics to beat them. Stephen's wife at home with their children stated that she 'slept better in her bed knowing that James Smeed, a trusted employee, would be a good companion for Stephen and look after his master well'.

In 1856, James was at Bunninyong, south of Ballarat and was a bullock driver. Then in 1872, his dearest friend, Stephen, died, aged just sixty one, in Victoria. James was devastated. He stayed on with the Henty's as a grieving, yet faithful retainer. He died in 1882 at Penola in South Australia, still living on land owned by the Henty's. He never married.

Charles Giles was a shoemaker from Bilsington. Born in 1797, his mother (Anne) was first cousin to John Bailey. In October 1818 Charles married Mary Chapman in St Rumwolds church in Bonnington. The fact that they both signed the register shows that they had both been educated to some degree. By the time he was transported, Charles and Mary had three daughters, Sarah, Jane and Annie Margaret.

Charles had been with the gang for about five years before he was captured. He was encouraged to get involved with the free trade by the easy money - always useful to a man with a growing family - and some gentle persuasion by his mother's cousin, John Bailey. He was taken in the early morning of the October 1826 arrests, but he had been involved in a near miss in the May of that year too.

He was one of a hundred and fifty smugglers, organised by George Ransley, who converged on the coast at Herring Hang. They fired on a party of preventative men pursuing them and those same duly fired back. Charles was wounded in the neck during the shoot-out and George ordered Edward Horne, (who later turned King's evidence against them) to carry him to the high road where George collected him in his cart and took him to his aunt's house at West Wall. George himself paid for Charles' medical care until he was healed. He ever afterwards passed off the scar as the 'effects of a blister'!

Within three months of arriving in the colony he was appointed to the field police at Campbell Town. He did not stay with the force for very long before he returned to his old profession as a shoemaker.

By January 1829 Charles' employer, James Grant Esq, wrote to ask permission for his assigned servant's wife and children to land that day. Mary and their daughters had sailed aboard the *Harmony* with other wives and children of some of the other gang members from Kent. His son, Charles Chapman Giles, was born barely nine months after Mary's arrival. In 1830 he was assigned to his wife and gained his ticket of leave in 1833. During those years two more daughters, Mary and Harriet were born.

Mary Giles senior became unwell and, despite Charles' care, and the skills of the Doctors, she died on the 12th of June 1839 aged just thirty nine and was buried at St David's Anglican burial ground, which was Hobart's first cemetery.

Charles held the family together but he was grieving and became withdrawn into himself. He failed to notice that Jane, his second daughter was becoming pale and was often ill in the mornings. Her waist was becoming thick. On the 27th of June 1841, Jane gave birth to a baby boy. She called him William Charles and would not reveal who the father was, but Charles suspected that it was his twenty two year old apprentice Samuel!

Charles snapped out of his slough of despond and took control. They registered the baby under the name of Giles and Jane and the baby continued to live with him - although they had separate quarters in the upper rooms of his house. In the census of 1843 Jane and baby William, by then two years old, are listed separately.

Jane started openly courting Samuel Quodrill, the former apprentice of Charles, who was, by then, a shoemaker in his own right. Jane would never say who William's father was, but he did look a lot like Sam. On the 3rd of January 1852 they were married. Jane was twenty nine. The couple went on to have three more children, Richard, born in 1859 - he died of gastric fever in 1889 aged thirty. Thomas was born in 1860 and died of rheumatic heart disease in 1882 aged twenty three. Amelia was born in 1865. Jane herself died of abdominal cancer in 1882 aged sixty two.

Charles continued on as a shoemaker, living with his son at 31 Harrington Street Hobart. A young, twenty three year old widow brought shoes in for repair and they struck up a friendship. Her name was Emma Stratton and she spent more time in his shop; he, in turn, took more pride in his appearance and looked forward to her visits. They spoke for hours and he let her into the secret of how he really came by the scars on his neck. They spoke of his exploits on the marshes and she relished his stories of the audacious scrapes with the Government excise men. He in turn heard of how she had nursed her husband through his final illness. One day he had a small posy of flowers waiting for her when she visited. As he presented it to her, he asked her if she would care to walk out with him the following Sunday afternoon. To his delight and amazement she agreed. Courtship followed and on the 16th of July 1856 he married her. He was fifty seven years old at the time.

No one, looking at the middle aged, respectable, Hobart shoe maker, would ever have imagined his past. Just thirty years previously he had been dodging the government excise men on the beaches and coves of Kent, the scars on his neck from a wound inflicted by a Government issued flintlock!

Emma and Charles went on to have more children between them. Robert was born in 1857, but died before his first birthday. Elizabeth was born in 1859 and Thomas in 1860. Finally Catherine was born in 1863. They had a few happy years until Charles suffered a stroke in the late spring of 1874. He lingered, partially paralysed, in pain and totally dependent on his wife and children. On September the 2nd 1874, he died. He was aged seventy six. He lies in Queenborough Cemetery, in Sandy Bay, which is a suburb of Hobart.

Within a year of arriving in the colony all our married Kentish men had applied for permission for their wives and family to join them.

Home Fires

And ever has it been known,

That love knows not its own depth

Until that hour of separation

(Khalil Gibran)

Back home in Aldington Frith Elizabeth Ransley – Bet - was angry! Really, really, frustratingly, steamingly, tremblingly, lividly angry! She had warned George a hundred times about allowing the youngsters to carry firearms. Her father would never have countenanced it! Samuel Senior (Thresher) always carried a threshing flail as a weapon on the free trade runs. "It's good to defend yourselves." he had said. "The Revenue men expect it; but to take up arms against King and country? It'll end in no good, mark my words!" Now his prophetic words had borne fruit. Fifty children in the villages had been left as good as orphaned; eleven wives without husbands - not to mention the widow of the poor young midshipman, Richard Morgan. He had been shot on Dover beach by a stray bullet fired by that young tear-arse, Dick Wire, if rumour was to be believed. She, herself, left here fighting to keep her own home from being taken by the officials and with ten children to care for. Matilda, now seventeen, was a help and her eldest sons - young George, sixteen, and John, fourteen, had been forced to go cap in hand to squire Deeds to try to get farm work to save them all from starving! The baby, Elizabeth, George had never even met! She was born whilst he languished at Portsmouth on some rotting prison hulk. Baby Betsy she called her, but she was always poorly. Bet blamed it on the stresses of her last few months of pregnancy after George and the others had been arrested.

It had been a freezing clear frosty night in October. At a little after 3am Bet was woken by Matilda screaming out 'warhorses'. That was the code word that told the household to be alert as the law was upon them. George sprang up immediately and was struggling into his breeches when they had heard heavy footsteps pounding up the wooden staircase. Bet just had time to wrap the sheet around herself and grab the chamber pot, which she was prepared to use on the head of Lieutenant Hellard, who was leading the party! The bedroom door was kicked open and two burly dragoons grabbed George by the arms and cuffed him before he could resist. She remembered screaming profanities whilst another soldier restrained her and then they had dragged George downstairs and outside. Leaning out of the bedroom window, Bet could see her two brothers, Robert and Samuel, the Wire brothers and Charles Giles, the shoemaker, already outside and ironed together. Dutchy and Tom Denard completed the ensemble. Within minutes they were being marched off by the soldiers in the direction of Hythe - a seven mile trek - bound for Fort Moncrief. As the sound of the party died away, Matilda's sobbing was the only sound to be heard as she stood over their two guard dogs motionless on the grass, their throats cruelly slit by Hellard's men! How Bet hated them all at that moment.

She sent young George to George's Cousin John at Mersham. He could petition Sir Edward Knatchbull to intervene. The Squire knew more about this than Bet herself did - up to his neck in it, she would swear. Now was the time for him to step in and save them if he could. Her widowed father, Samuel senior, (Thresher) came over to fix her door and comfort them as best he could; but he had also lost two sons, as well as George, to the law. At that point they were aware that the offences they might be charged with carried the death sentence!

On a very stormy night of torrential rain in November the troops were back once more in Aldington village. The remaining gang members had taken to sleeping rough in barns and outhouses so as to avoid the law; but Hellard's men seemed to know just where to go just as they had (mysteriously) known which houses to surround in the October raids. That night several more of the gang were rounded up; these included Bet's Uncle, John Bailey —he was also Thresher's younger half-brother, and Paul Pierce. Paul had escaped the October raids by hiding up the chimney of his ancient house in Bonnington. He had installed a brick step for just such an occasion. However, it helped him not a whit in that November raid. Edward Pantry, nephew to her brother Samuel's wife Sarah, plus James Quested, then her brother-in-law, Richard Higgins, Thomas Wheeler (the blacksmith from Folkestone), James Smeed, James Hogben, James Wilson and John Horne. James Smeed's brother, Thomas, also a gang member had been ignored and nobody gave him away so he was able to stay to support their parents.

Pantry and Horne had turned King's evidence at the very first opportunity. These traitors, as one might imagine, created some problems between her brother, Samuel, and his wife Sarah. A former gang member, James Spratford, had led Hellard and his men to the fugitives; apparently out of sheer greed for the reward money. For this action he was universally hated and was forced to shop outside of the village boundaries since none of the locals would either talk to him or serve him goods. Indeed, the village barber gave it out that he would sooner cut Spratford's throat than shave his beard! Thomas Wheeler and Bet's brother, Robert, were acquitted and walked free. The remaining fourteen of the gang who were tried, were sentenced to death. By the grace of God - and thanks to the intervention of Squire Knatchbull, who knew the solicitor general - this sentence had been commuted to transportation for life!

They were sent off to the prison hulks where poor James Wilson succumbed to the consumption. After just a few weeks she was told that they had been put aboard the *Governor Ready* and were bound for Van Diemen's Land. She hadn't seen George, or her kin, privately since that fateful night. She had attended the court case at Maidstone, so had seen him from the gallery, but George hadn't yet met his little daughter, Elizabeth.

Since the child's birth in the February of the previous year, Elizabeth had been sickly, with frequent purging and colic. Bet became a regular visitor to the village apothecary for opium and arrowroot. Dr Ralph Hougham had been over from Brookland on more than one occasion to administer astringent enemas and a flannel roller to the child's abdomen. Despite his worthy ministrations she continued to be a poor doer, and remained underweight and in poor health.

Bet's pleading with Squire Knatchbull had secured the roof over their heads for the time being, but not all of her neighbours had fared so well. Many of the wives and families were being kept by the parish and the workhouse loomed menacingly over each one of them.

She had learned from Mr Platt, the family solicitor, that George had successfully petitioned for her and the children, to join him out there.

How angry she was with George! She hated him, yet she loved him. She could cheerfully throttle him, yet she longed to fall into his arms! Why should she leave her family, her brother Robert, her aging, widowed, father and all of her friends in Kent to travel to the other side of the world? She had heard bad things about the dangers there; poisonous snakes, deadly spiders and such like - not to mention the indigenous people resenting the new settlers. It was said that they ambushed strangers - killing the men, stealing the children away and Lord knew what else they did to the women! But, then again, her sister, Rhoda, and her children would be going, and possibly her sister-in-law, Sarah, and Catherine, her aunt, with her six children. She was not sure if Sarah would go. She hadn't forgiven Samuel for getting caught and leaving them. Most of her friends from the village would be travelling though. Almost more of her kin would be out there than here at home in Kent; but she was still seething mad at George for being caught and leaving her to cope all alone.

In anger she kicked the chair as she rose to pour herself a cup of tea. Even that was getting short in supply - along with her favourite gin! She cursed aloud when she saw how low the tea caddy was, and slammed the kettle back down on the range. The noise woke baby Betsy who set up her weak irritating bawling. "Damn and blast!" cursed Bet, and headed for the wooden cradle.

Sarah Bailey was with her aunt Catherine. Sarah had been Sarah Pantry until her marriage to Samuel Bailey in 1808. They had a young daughter called Ann. Catherine was married to Samuel's uncle John - although Catherine and

John were some ten years younger than their nephew, Samuel, and herself - they had six children. Sarah's nephew, Edward Pantry, had been a member of the blues. Captured in the November raids, he had been sleeping in an old outhouse on a farm in an attempt to avoid detection. He very soon turned Kings evidence to try to save himself. This had caused much resentment from the other members of the gang, not to mention the locals. It also caused trouble between Sarah and Samuel since Sarah took her nephew's side. On her one visit to see Samuel in Maidstone gaol they had argued about it. The few letters exchanged between them had been acrimonious. Edward Horne, who had also turned King's evidence, had been caught for horse theft and transported to New South Wales even before Samuel and the rest of the gang had left the prison hulks! Out for revenge on Edward Pantry, the locals took to watching his every move. At the end of the February, after the rest of the gang were taken to the hulks, Huggins Higgins, brother to Richard Higgins (and yes, that really was his name!) saw him stealing two sheep from a farm in Bonnington. An unspoken honour amongst villains would normally have protected Edward, but he himself had broken that by turning against his fellow smugglers. Huggins rounded up about twenty villagers plus

Constable Stokes. They surrounded his cottage and the constable, along with two burly fellows, went inside. There they found two sheepskins and some remains. Edward Pantry was on the prison hulks by the 24th of March and on 16th of October in 1827 he was transported for life to New South Wales on the aptly named *Retribution.*

No one, except his family, missed him in Aldington and the surrounding villages. They all thought the name of the ship most appropriate for his journey! This had made Sarah very bitter but Samuel was delighted. His parents, Sarah's brother and sister-in-law, were, however, grieving for him. Sarah missed him too and felt sorry for her brother. Now they had been told that they could join their husbands - indeed they should join them - as the parish would no longer support them. They would pay for their passage out to the colony and also for that of their children. Catherine had told Sarah that in just four short months the *Harmony* would be sailing from Downs dock, near Gravesend. They would all be leaving together aboard her. Sarah didn't want to go. She, like most of the wives, was still angry with her husband. How could he allow them to get into this mess? It had been hell this past eighteen months - struggling on just a meagre hand-out from the parish and with a little help from her family. The

Baileys fortunes were dwindling with no free trade to boost it. It seemed that they always needed something that she could ill afford. The nights were peaceful though; the bed spacious and quiet without Samuel snatching all the blankets and snoring beside her! Oh, she wanted to stay; but was the workhouse the only choice if she did? Catherine had been encouraging. "They have good jobs and are building nice houses for us. It will be a whole new life and a fresh start away from this hellhole." was what she had told her. She supposed that she had no choice, or did she? Her brother at Elham had offered her and Ann a home with him. There was now more space in it since Edward had been transported. She would make Samuel suffer though. She would not tell him if she was joining him or not until the very last minute and, if she did decide to go, she would tell him that she hoped he had built her a separate bedroom in that new house of his; or, preferably, a separate house all together!

Frances Gilham was worried. She had recently given birth to a daughter whom she also called Frances. By the time they sailed the baby would be a mere five months old and just eight months or so when they arrived in the colony. What would Thomas say? He had been gone from her since

October 1826 and now it was May '28. Even his poor grasp of numbers would show that they had been apart for some ten months before the girl's conception! But then again, he couldn't know what a struggle she had had with all of the children. Yes, it had certainly been a hard task to feed them and keep them clothed, albeit poorly and in each other's hand-me-downs.

He had been handsome, the visiting journeyman. He was staying at the Walnut Tree inn and had called by to offer his wares - packs of pins and pretty ribbons. She had protested that she had nothing to spare for fripperies such as he was offering. He had, despite her protests, held a fetching blue ribbon to her hair and told her how beautiful it looked and how it matched her eyes. She felt flattered. He was handsome. She was lonely and, well, things got out of hand when he produced the bottle of Geneva! He did leave a very generous price of his board under his pillow when he departed the following morning, but she had no idea how to trace him or where he lived. Her only option - other than the workhouse - was to turn up and throw herself on Thomas' mercy. Perhaps she wouldn't tell him about little Frances before she arrived though! She knew Mary Giles would be going, and Rhoda Higgins and Bet Ransley. She thought the

Bailey wives would be leaving too - although Sarah Bailey seemed to be, as yet, undecided.

Sarah Pierce had been dealing with tragedy. Their baby, Charles, who was just over a year old, had died while his father was at sea and on his way to the colony. To add to her grief, and only three days after the *Governor Ready* docked in Hobart, their daughter, Celia - known as Seeley – died. She was seven years old.

Sarah Pierce had decided that she was going out there in any case, but her friends all feared for her since she had the voyage to arrange, with all of its complications, while she was in such deep sorrow.

Ann Hogben was having tea with the wife of her husband's cousin, Jane Quested, wife of James Quested. "I hear the others are leaving in October. It will be quiet around here without them." She had said. Jane felt sorry for her. Her husband, James Hogben, had tried to escape - unsuccessfully, as in everything else he attempted! For that he was refused permission to bring his wife and family out. "He can apply again in another year or so." Jane had told Ann. "I have not yet heard from my James, so I shall not be going with the others; that is if he wants me out there at all! He cannot be all that keen or he would already have applied for me to join him. Well, he can wait now. I will travel with you if and when you go. I do not fancy that long journey to Lord knows where on my own." Ann smiled and patted her friend's elbow; "Thank you for that Jane, my dear." she had said and poured them both a second cup of tea.

In Harmony

There is a tide in the affairs of men, which taken at the flood, leads on to fortune. Omitted, all the voyage of their life is bound in shallows and miseries. On such a full sea are we now afloat. And we must take the current when it serves, or lose our ventures.

(William Shakespeare)

It was a hard decision for the wives to leave all they had ever known and venture forth into the unknown new world. Due to constrictions of space they could only take limited baggage. This meant that they could take just basic clothing for themselves and their children, and only the smallest and most valuable trinkets could travel with them.

The parish had paid for most of them - Rhoda Higgins and her children included. It was not common knowledge, but Bet and her children had been paid for by Sir Edward Knatchbull. The Baileys had pooled resources to pay for Catherine and her children. Houses had been packed up, belongings sold, or given to relatives. George's favourite horse was sold to his cousin, John; and his cousin, George, at Ivychurch, bought his cart and harness. Sentimental trinkets too large to take had to be left behind or given away to friends. It was a sad and unsettled time but, finally, the women of the village set off for Gravesend. Robert Bailey, his brother William and their father, Samuel senior, packed their carts with Bet, Rhoda Higgins and Catherine plus their children - eighteen between them. Sarah had decided not to leave Kent. It was, therefore, with much sorrow (and knowing that Samuel would be devastated), that they said goodbye to her.

Travelling out to the colony were, Elizabeth Ransley (ten children), Rhoda Higgins (two children), Catherine Bailey (six children), Mary Giles (three children), Frances Gilham (six children), and Sarah Pierce (five children, having lost two). There were two other free women travellers with another child and a hundred female convicts all set to board the *Harmony*.

They saw her as soon as the waggons turned into the harbour. She stood impressive - 373 tonnes and white sails gleaming in the autumn sun. Built at St Johns, her Master was Bennett Ireland. Her surgeon superintendent was William Clifford. Bet made a note of that, for Betsy was poorly again. Bet knew that she would be seeing the ship's surgeon on a regular basis.

Farewells are tiresome. No one wants to take permanent leave of their loved ones. No amount of hugging or final kisses can take away the heartache and emptiness of parting, so they made the best they could of it, promising to write regularly. They then went down below decks to their berths - their homes for the next four months or so. The weather was set fair so, a few days later, the *Harmony* set sail for Van Diemen's Land. This was on the 13th of September 1828.

Little Elizabeth continued to purge and be poorly. Bet was exhausted through lack of sleep. On the 25th of September an unrelated, but sad, event occurred. Josh Neil, the ten month old baby of one of the convict women, died. He had been purging and was undernourished and emaciated. They buried him at sea. Bet felt some foreboding about little Betsy's health.

On the 2nd of October, Rhoda Higgins, Bet's sister, was admitted to the ships hospital with dysentery and a gastric fever. Warm baths, flannel rollers to the abdomen, rice water to drink and a diet of sago and soup seemed to improve her. Calomel and opium finally worked and she was discharged as being well again on the 12th of October. Bet and Catherine Bailey had been looking after her children all the time she was incapacitated.

The ship continued to plough the waves. Bet became worn down. Little Betsy continued to do badly. On the 10th of October, when they were just off the Isle of Jago, she was admitted to the ship's hospital. It was her old problem of swollen belly and purging of the bowels. Surgeon Clifford reported that she had not been well since embarking on board of the ship. She was suffering swollen glands and abdomen, much debility and loss of appetite. Her abdomen caused her much pain on pressure and she had constant purging of the bowels. Surgeon Clifford treated her with warm baths, flannel rollers to the abdomen, sago, astringent enemas and opium plus arrowroot. By the 14th she was passing blood, by the 15th, she was refusing all food and medication, was in pain and had a high temperature. By the 17th, she had a mucus discharge from the bowel and had a black crustation of the tongue (*the wording is taken from contemporary medical reports*). Poor little Betsy died at 4pm on the 18th of October. They buried her at sea. She was just twenty months old and had never even met her father! Poor Bet was distraught, but found comfort in having family and friends aboard to support her. Rhoda and Catherine Bailey, her sister in law, spent their time in comforting her and looking after her other children.

Sarah Pierce also became unwell with swollen inflamed eyes and discomfort when looking at the light. She was admitted to the ship's hospital on the 24th of October. Her constitution was worn down by grief for her deceased children. She had a high temperature, a rapid pulse, shivers and a great thirst. Clifford put her on a light diet, bled her twelve ounces of blood, put in eye drops and insisted that she rest. By the 25th she had loose bowels and her eyes were worse, with much discharge. Clifford flushed warm fomentations between her eyelids and put lint between them to absorb the discharge. By the 31st there was visible improvement of the eyes and less pain. Sarah recovered slowly and was discharged as being well on the 12th of November.

It seemed that Sarah Pierce had company in the hospital for part of her stay as, on 27th October, Rhoda Higgins was readmitted complaining of lack of sleep and energy, debility, florid tongue and pain in the chest. She complained of being unable to eat the ship's food as it was lacking in the milk and vegetables to which she was accustomed! Kindly Surgeon Clifford very patiently procured

94

for her some fresh meat and vegetables from the Captain's provisions. He gave her hospital soup with wine and a decoction of bark with quassiae. By the 29th she was sleeping better and gaining strength. She seemed to enjoy the wine diet, and the bark treatment was continued. She was discharged as well on the 6th of November.

Their wearisome voyage continued. They all suffered bouts of sea sickness as well as homesickness. Each and every one of them longed for land and the reunion with their husbands (if only to break the monotony of the daily ship routine).

Sarah Pierce continued to have intermittent fevers and chronic hepatitis. On December the 2nd she started vomiting and suffered bowel spasms. She was, once again, admitted to the hospital, where she was treated with sago and rain water diet, flannel rollers to the abdomen and calomel and opium. By the 5th she had tenderness over the liver and a sore mouth. Soup and wine was added to her diet. By the 7th she had improved and was discharged as well on the 18th of December.

On the 7th of January sixteen year old George, eldest son of George and Bet, was taken into the hospital with conjunctivitis. The treatment of warm flushes and lint to the eyelids proved to be successful and he was discharged well on the 10th of January. They were just off the coast of Van Diemen's Land.

At long last The *Harmony* docked. By now it was the 14th of January 1829, and the ship had been at sea for one hundred and twenty three days. There had only been the loss of the two children's lives.

Apart from a virulent conjunctivitis on board and certain other odd ailments, Surgeon Clifford landed his charges in general good health. He attributed this to keeping the ship extremely clean and well ventilated, encouraging the women to spend as much time as possible up on deck and providing regular meals and daily personal examination of the women and children in his care.

Reunited

It takes one person to forgive

It takes two people to be reunited

(Lewis B Smedes)

Sarah Pierce was somewhat apprehensive as she waited for Paul to come and collect her. How would he react to seeing his family minus young Seeley and baby Charles? She, herself, had aged and lost a fair amount of weight through illness and grief. Paul's application for his family to join him had been approved by Governor Arthur on the 24th of November 1828, but Sarah and the children had set sail in the September of that year - one month before Paul had submitted his application! The Pierce's went off to Paul's employer, John Burnett Esq., in Hobart.

Gradually the men arrived from the interior to claim their families. All the women feared the initial meeting with their respective loved ones for a variety of reasons. Samuel Bailey came to greet his sisters. He had applied for permission for Sarah and Ann to join him, but Rhoda had written to warn him that they wouldn't be accompanying them on the voyage. He, Samuel, was assigned to Edward Bisdee Esq. He valued Samuel's work, and he in turn, respected his employer and was happy working his seven hundred acres of land in Melton Mowbray. Bisdee came from Somerset in England and so was sympathetic to Samuel's homesickness. Samuel was to stay with him for many years. Bet and Rhoda were full of sympathy for him not having his family arrive with the rest of them. He half hoped that Sarah would have changed her mind at the last minute and would be aboard with the others. She had not. He put on a brave face, but, inside, felt completely broken.

George and Bet's reunion was tinged with the heartbreak of losing little Betsy, but George, having never known her, whilst sad, was still overjoyed to see the rest of his family. John Bailey and Charles Giles rushed to the docks to meet their families. There were many tears and hugs exchanged. Within days all were off the boat and travelling to the interior with their loved ones; all, that is, except Rhoda Higgins and Frances Gilham. These ladies waited for their spouses to arrive to collect them. Daily they scanned the docks for any sign of their menfolk, but still they did not come!

On the 24th of January – ten days after the ship had docked - William Clifford, the surgeon wrote to the Colonial Secretary to inform him that the two women were still on board. Richard Higgins was in the service of Samuel Hill at Campbell Town. He was the first to arrive following the Colonial Secretary's involvement and Rhoda and the children left with him on the 5th of February. Rhoda reassured Frances that Thomas would arrive soon and promised that they would not abandon her if he failed to do so. Nonetheless, she was wracked with anxiety.

Frances Gilham and her six children were about to be sent to the Female Factory - an institution for female convicts and their children in Hobart – when, on the 7th of February, Thomas finally arrived from the interior to collect them. He explained his failure to arrive beforehand as 'an inability to procure a conveyance for them to his master's place of residence'!

Captain Ireland was eager to depart. *The Harmony* had another mission to begin. The failure of Richard and Thomas to collect their families had caused a twenty one day delay in the ship's departure!

Frances had thought that she and the children had been abandoned. She had not told Thomas about baby Frances. She had thought to fling herself upon his mercy once they had been reunited. She had not bargained on the news reaching him in advance. She realised that, in all probability, one of the other wives (possibly Bet Ransley, or Catherine Bailey) had told their husbands, who had forewarned Thomas. Was that the reason he did not come? Had he abandoned her? How would they manage in the Female Factory? Would he forgive her?

When they had first married he had gained an instant family; she already had three children out of wedlock. She knew what the other village women said about her, but she always thought Thomas loved her. Finally, when he arrived, their meeting was tense. Thomas stood in silence for what seemed like an age to Frances. After several tense entreaties, her tears and expressions of how much she had missed him and how hard things had been without his income, brought him round. A frosty truce was called between them. Frances kept her head down and, for many weeks, paid extra attention to her wifely duties. Little Frances was brought up and accepted as any other Gilham child (although, she and Frances' three eldest children were not included in Thomas' will).

They finally settled to their new life in Norfolk Plains. George and Bet Ransley, with their nine surviving children, went back to the upper Derwent; to his employer, Mr Thompson, at Charlie's Hope. George had applied to build a wooden house for his family, as had most of the Kentish men. They were given a quarter acre plot - which they rented. The house had to be built to a certain specification. These had to be thirty by sixteen feet with a picket fence surrounding them. They also had to be completed within three months of permission being granted. George had almost finished his building work when Bet and the children arrived. Life took a lot of adjusting to for Bet and the Ransley children. Compared to their lives in Kent, life here was primitive, hard and they were short on luxuries; however, the joy of being together again outweighed these inconveniences. George worked long hours sometimes - not only at his public works for Mr Thompson, but in farming a little for himself. He rented acreage, at two shillings per hundred acres, to make extra cash to support them. During these times, Bet was glad of the company of Matilda and her other children. She was pleased that she had family nearby also. George was, as yet, still living in quarters provided by his employer (officially) although he did stay with Bet and his family on occasions.

Yes, life could certainly be lonely here in this new land.. At times Bet missed her father and other brothers and she wished that she had never left Kent. At other times, when George was with her, she knew she could live anywhere in the world just as long as they were together.

The house was finished and, in 1830, George was assigned to Bet (meaning that he could officially live with her). At this time their household comprised of Matilda aged twenty, George aged nineteen, John aged eighteen, William fourteen, Robert twelve, James ten, Ann eight, Edward seven and Hannah aged five.

In that year, 1830, most of the married lads from Kent were assigned to their wives. There were two exceptions. James Hogben had attempted an unsuccessful escape and so had to wait an extra year for permission to be granted for Ann to join him. Hogben's cousin, James Quested was the second. His wife, Jane, had opted to wait and travel with Ann Hogben and their children. Samuel Bailey, Bet's brother, was missing his wife and daughter, but was kept busy working for Edward Bisdee. The Wire brothers and James Smeed were unmarried. Bet (and Samuel's) uncle, John Bailey, was the brother-in-law of Thomas Gilham; they had married half-sisters. In later years, John's son, William, would marry Maria Gilham, daughter of Thomas and Frances, but in 1830 he was living and working near Sorell in New Norfolk. It was here that his daughter, Mary, met, and later married, Thomas Bennett, a convict from the *Arab* transport ship.

Not long afterwards Thomas fell foul of the law again and he and his wife were forced to flee to Adelaide in South Australia.

Ann Hogben and Jane Quested, along with their ten children between them, had safely landed in Hobart on the *Mellish* on the 22nd of September 1830. Ann Hogben had arrived with William aged thirteen, John twelve, James eleven, Susanna nine, and Ann aged eight. Mary Ann who was aged eighteen and Thomas, sixteen, remained in Kent in their respective work positions. In 1832 Ann and James were to have another son, Stephen, but he died aged just five months.

James Hogben, at this time, was assigned to J. C. Simpson Esq, Justice of the Peace and Police Magistrate for Campbell Town, so he lived fairly close to Richard and Rhoda Higgins. James Quested was assigned to Dr Francis Desaily, a medical officer from England, who had land at Jericho, Oatlands. Jane brought with her, James aged nine. He later became the captain of a schooner. Then she had Isabella, who was eight, and Theophillus, aged six. He went on to become a schoolmaster. Her two youngest were Jane at five and Sarah, who was just three years old. At that time Oatlands was still largely a building site situated on the plains. Jane Quested wondered what she had come to! It took her slightly longer than the other wives to settle in completely, but Dr Desaily proved to be a fair boss and they were tolerably comfortable.

Richard and Rhoda Higgins were living at Campbell Town and Richard was working at Gadesden - the estate of Justice of the Peace, Samuel Hill Esq. They were quite pleased to have Samuel Bailey, the Hogbens and the Quested's as near neighbours.

The Aldington families were justly proud in 1835 when they heard about James Smeed's heroism in capturing the two notorious bushrangers, Jeffkins and Brown. Previously they had heard that he had been dismissed from the police force in 1831 for his 'disobedience of orders'. Now, suddenly, he was a hero with half an entire page of newsprint in the Hobart Courier and a free pardon from the Governor of the colony.

It seemed that any man could achieve anything he wanted to in this strange new world if he worked hard enough for it!

George knew, from his observation of James Smeed's reckless disregard for his own safety back home in Kent, that he would either achieve great things, or end up prematurely dead! Most of our men had their 'tickets of leave' by 1833. As always there were exceptions. The Wire brothers, Samuel Bailey and James Hogben gained theirs in 1835.

George, John Bailey, Thomas Dennard and Charles Giles were given a conditional discharge in 1838 and all of the rest of the gang had to wait until 1839. They all gained their free pardons in 1841 except for James Hogben - who had to wait until 1843 for his, due to his escape attempt. Ann never really forgave him for that.

In June 1837 Samuel Bailey decided that he wanted to marry again. He had been apart from Sarah for ten years, and he construed her failure to join him as desertion. He went to the female factory and chose Hannah Evans. She was a female convict who had come to the colony on the *William Bryan*. At that time single females in the colony were scarce. The women were encouraged to marry since it eased the financial burden on the Government if a husband took them on. If a man wanted a wife he could go to the female factory where, every morning, women who wanted a husband to provide for them would stand in a line to be inspected by the men. If a man wanted one as his wife he dropped his handkerchief at her feet. If she picked it up it meant she accepted him and they would seek permission from the Governor's office to marry. Permission was granted to Samuel and Hannah on the proviso that the clergy agreed. They did not! Sarah Bailey was still living - albeit in Kent - so Samuel was not free in the eyes of the church! Much to his chagrin, Hannah Evans eventually married someone else.

Once more, in August 1841, after gaining his pardon, Samuel went to the female factory and chose Ruth Harris this time. She had come over on the *Hector*. Once more permission was refused (which seemed very harsh). Ruth married elsewhere and an increasingly bitter Samuel continued his lonely existence. Finally, in 1848, he took up lodgings with a widow. She was a free woman some six years younger than himself. Susan Nettlefold and Samuel got along famously, but marriage for Samuel was, at that point, out of the question as it seemed he was not considered a free man by the authorities. The couple co-habited without the benefit of the church. Finally, in 1854, Sarah, his estranged wife - who was some years older than Samuel - died in Kent at the age of seventy four! The news of her death took a further year to reach Samuel. He was happy to continue co-habiting, but Susan had other ideas! However, it took another eight years (1863) before he eventually gave in. He and Susan Nettlefold were married at Oatlands on the 24th of July. He was aged seventy three and she was sixty five!

George had gained his ticket of leave in 1833 and started renting his own land to farm, although he still did some work for the Government until his conditional discharge in 1838. He then rented extra land at Hollow Tree, near Kangaroo Point. He and his family continued to live in the Falls area of New Norfolk near Styx. In 1841 he was given his free pardon and received a letter from James Smeed. It said that James' brother Thomas - now married with children - and his family were coming out to the colony as free settlers and wanted work. George needed extra help as his lands now extended to some five hundred acres. He wrote back, reassuring James that his brother and family would be employed by him.

Thus it was, on the 10th of October 1842, the *Apolline* sailed into Hobart bringing Thomas and his family to the colony. The party consisted of Thomas himself who was aged thirty six and listed as a first class farm servant; his wife, Mary, twenty seven, was listed as a dairy servant. The children were son's Samuel aged ten and listed as being able to drive horses, then James, eight, and daughters Sarah, five, and Emma three. On October the 28th George arrived in Hobart to collect them. The reunion - after an absence of some sixteen years - was a very happy affair. George employed Thomas as a farm servant on a wage of £52 a year without rations to work his land at Hollow Tree. He also took Thomas Knights, from the same ship, with his wife Sarah and two children (Thomas Henry aged eight and George just two). The Knights and the Smeeds were of similar age and had become friendly on board the *Apolline*. James Smeed had promised Thomas Knights that he would put in a good word for him with George. They were delighted for Thomas to be taken on as farm servant at a wage of eight shillings a week plus board and lodging. George was becoming a man of substance again.

Earning their Freedom

'Freedom is the power to choose our own chains'

Jean Jaques Rousseau

Life was turning out well for the families from Kent. Generally their standard of living was better than they might have had back home if they had kept on the right side of the law. Gradually all of George and Bet's children married, moved out of the family home into homes of their own and had children. Many of them became employers themselves.

George Junior was the first, when he married Bridget Murrell on the 1st of June 1831. They wed at New Norfolk in the parish of River Styx and both signed their names, as they were both literate. They went on to have six daughters and eight sons, but lost a daughter and two sons in infancy and a son aged just six years. One of their sons, William George, known mostly as George, married a Georgina Raynor in 1868. They were deeply in love and very happy. They went on to have children, but their happiness was short lived. In 1878, their twin babies died and then, on the 18th of September 1879 Georgina herself died from rheumatic fever. She was aged just thirty one years and is buried at Bushy Park with her twin babies. William George never recovered from her loss and did not remarry.

Matilda was the next to fly the nest when she married Charles Fenton on the 6th of May 1833 at Falls, New Norfolk. The Fentons were a big family who employed convict workers themselves. Despite that, Charles could neither read nor write (unlike Mattie, who was literate). At that time there was not the basic infrastructure in the colony to provide education for the masses.

They moved to Fenton Forest and had eleven children, eight of which survived.

William married next - one Janet Robinson in Fenton Forest on the 12th of November 1836. Matilda and Charles were the witnesses. Then Robert wed Margaret Lobdale on the 28th of March 1838. They produced ten children. Anne married William Gundry on the 24th of June 1839. They went on to have eleven surviving children. George and Bet seemed to have an offspring's wedding every year! John, their third born and second son, married Mary Salter on the 6th of February 1841. She was eighteen years old, ten years younger than he was. They married in St Matthew's Church, New Norfolk and went on to have seventeen children. Of these, ten girls and four boys survived to adulthood.

Tragically, they lost a son, William, aged just four when his clothes caught fire as he played near a field of burning stubble with another boy. He died of his burns. One of their boys (John) was born on the 13th of February 1852 at New Norfolk. He was significant; but more of him later.

Hannah Ransley married next, on the 5th of October 1848 to George Halyer Rayner at Hobart, they produced twelve surviving children.

James aged twenty six, married a forty three year old widow, Marianne William, at Hamilton on the 15th of February 1849. Finally Edward, who was aged twenty five married the sixteen year old Elizabeth Higgins - a cousin - on the 2nd of May 1850. John Pool (at that time her stepfather), Bet Ransley and John's married sister, Hannah, were witnesses at the wedding. They went on to have four children.

With their family grown so large, George and Bet were growing rich in human terms, albeit somewhat poorer financially!

Thomas and Frances Gilham settled at Longford, where they went on to have seven more children. They did, however, lose one (a daughter) at five months old in 1830. In February

1831 Delia, then sixteen, married George McDonald who had been transported from Wiltshire aboard the *Dromedary*. They also settled in Longford and their first child, George, was born in October 1832. Frances went on to have twins and four more children and Delia ended up having six children, hopefully they were able to help each other.

Thomas ended up buying property and building a substantial portfolio. He rented several hundred acres at Westbury from William Bryan at twelve shillings and sixpence per acre.

In the 1850's his sons started to marry, leaving him short of farming labour, so he turned his investments into residential properties. By 1853 the family lived at Patterson Plains just outside Launceston - later known as St Leonards. They had forty eight acres, a large dwelling with stables and a school room. In 1854 they moved to Westbury, where he owned two properties. His annual income from his properties at that time was substantial.

By 1856, Thomas was the licensee of the 'Jolly Farmer', later known as 'the Prince of Wales Inn' at Carrick. The inn had been built around 1840. It had become an important coaching inn and change station for horses. It also boasted overnight accommodation for weary travellers. The inn had sixteen rooms, a skittle alley and accommodation for thirty horses. By 1858 Thomas owned various properties in Carrick and Westbury. His daughter, Louisa, had died in 1848 from a fever aged just twenty-three. Her husband had died in 1852 and so their three young boys were brought up by Frances and Thomas. When Thomas died from 'natural decay' on the 15th of May 1865, he left his property portfolio to his wife and, on her demise, to his children and the children of his dead daughter, Louisa. He was sixty two. Frances made her will out to divide all of her own savings since Thomas' death to all of her children on her demise. Frances died in 1869 and in 1870 most of the Gilham properties were sold off and the proceeds divided between the Gilham children.

Thomas 'Dutchy' Gilham was undoubtedly the wealthiest of the Aldington gang and yet he had been one of the toughest of them in their heyday and could neither read nor write his own name.

Paul and Sarah Pierce went on to have Alfred in July 1830 followed, some years later, by their youngest son, Henry Deblaine Pierce. By 1842, it would appear that they were living apart since Paul was living on his own in Hobart with

Alfred and Henry. Sarah died (also in Hobart) in 1848 of consumption. By 1864 Paul had numerous grandchildren. Paul himself died on the 18th of October 1864 aged eighty. He died at home in Brisbane Street.

Richard and Rhoda Higgins brought their two daughters over to the colony when Jane was seven and Mary just two. Martha was born later in the year that Rhoda had arrived (1829) and Richard was born in October 1832. Elizabeth arrived in 1834 and John in 1836. They were living at Green Ponds at that time. This changed, in 1837, when Richard was accused of sheep stealing. He was pardoned, but sent to live in Morven. This caused him to drink more than was seemly for, in 1839, he was fined for drunkenness. On the 15th of May 1839, he was granted a conditional pardon and gained his free pardon in 1841.

Their happiness was to be short lived, however. George Ransley came home from the fields on Wednesday afternoon, the 18th of August 1841. He burst through the door calling to Bet about next year's crop in the bottom field, to find Rhoda sitting at the kitchen table, her hands over her face and her shoulders shaking. Bet had her arms around her sister's shoulders and Samuel Bailey was standing in front of the window, gazing out with a distracted look in his eyes and his hands in his pockets. George fell silent at once as Bet shot him a warning look. "Richard has been killed!" She told him. George felt as though he had been sandbagged.

It appears that the previous Monday, the 16th of August, Richard - by now a small farmer - had been to Tea Tree, between Brighton and Richmond, to meet a prospective buyer for his crops. Richard liked a drink. Rhoda could not be certain, but it was highly likely that he had consumed more than was good for him and failed to hear the cart which came at breakneck speed round the corner just as Richard was crossing the road. The horse was flat out at trot. The driver yelled out and Richard saw them at the last minute. He jumped back and missed the horse, but fell. The metal cart wheels passed right over his chest crushing his ribs and piercing his lungs. He lingered briefly and was taken to a nearby house where a doctor attended him, but he died within hours. Rhoda had only heard the news the following day.

She had sent Jane to get Samuel while she packed an overnight bag for herself and her two youngest. They then left Jane and her husband, Joseph Wright, in charge of the other children while they left for George and Bet's house. Rhoda wanted her older sister at that time!

This was a sad time. On the Thursday, the 19th, the children were left with Matilda and Charles to play with their cousins while Rhoda, Samuel and Bet went to the mortuary to view Richard's poor broken body. The Inquest took place at Richmond on Friday the 20th of August. The Coroner, Frederick South, recorded a verdict of 'Accidental Death by the wheel of a cart passing over his body'. That was the end of poor Richard! He was forty-five years old.

His death was formally registered with John Abbott, Deputy Registrar, on the 6th of September 1841. George and Bet were of some comfort to Rhoda, but she was a worried woman. Richard had left her in considerable debt.

Bet and George discussed it. "You know I will not see her and the children starve," George told Bet, "but we are not as flush as we used to be back home in the old days. I can help a little financially but I have overheads, rent and staff to pay, as well as keeping the wolf from our own door." George had been saddened by the death of his friend. He thought back to their days in Kent. Their night runs to the beaches at Dymchurch and Camber. Richard had never been the bravest of the gang, but he was totally reliable and loyal to his fellow gang members. What a waste of a life. He was taken too soon, George lamented.

Rhoda defaulted on the mortgage payments, the pressure was on and finally she realised that she had no choice but to sell off some land. Ten acres of their Campbell Town farm was auctioned off in the November of 1841 to clear the mortgage default debts. It took some of the pressure off, but things were very tight. Rhoda, already a 'thin woman of yellowish habit' (as described by Surgeon Clifford on the *Harmony*), became even thinner and more sallow!

For a few years she concentrated on bringing up her family and making sure they all had food on the table. She frequently visited New Norfolk, to see her sister and nieces and nephews. On one such visit she met a neighbour of Matilda and Charles. He was an itinerant worker, working for Charles. John Pool had come over in 1826 on the *Andromeda* from London aged just twenty. He was a total rebel and yet was resourceful. He had given the authorities nothing but trouble by absconding, riotous behaviour, violence and drunkenness. He had spent time in Port Arthur (which, at that time was a penal settlement and included a huge penitentiary and its own church built by convicts). He had also worked on the chain gangs. He had suffered frequent lashings and solitary confinement. Finally, after many years in the colony, he gained his ticket of leave, followed by his conditional pardon. He travelled around getting work wherever he could. He and Rhoda got on very well. He wanted a wife, she wanted a provider and they both wanted companionship. On the 12th of November 1846 they married in St Matthew's Church, New Norfolk. He was forty years old and she was forty six. He was able to sign the register with his signature so he was, despite his rebelliousness, literate. Rhoda signed with her mark since she was not. Robert Ransley, her nephew, and his wife Margaret, were witnesses. Charles Fenton gave John permanent work in Fenton Forest and a wooden house to live in. Rhoda rented her house at Oatlands to her eldest, Jane, and her husband and thus life became less of a struggle for them all.

After some years they moved back to Oatlands - to Hilly Park - where Rhoda died on the 24th of October 1862 aged 66 from bronchitis. She was listed on her death certificate as the wife of a farmer. John stayed on there until he died in 1888; in his will he left the property to Rhoda's grandson, Stephen.

John and Catherine Bailey's family had also grown. Daughter Mary, as already stated, had married Thomas Gard in June 1831. No record of daughter, Catherine, marrying could be found, but their daughter, Elizabeth, married Robert Williams, whose father, William Williams, had come over from England on the *Calcutta*. They had married in Hobart on the 15th of August 1837. Emily married Thomas Piety who was a convict who had arrived aboard the *Georgiana* in 1829. They also married in Hobart but on the 14th of November 1842. It is believed that John junior married Fanny Remy Kenny, an Irish immigrant, in 1856. They went on to have three daughters and a son, Samuel. William was married and then widowed. It is believed he married a lady called Sarah who was some years older than himself. She died from 'delirium tremens' aged forty nine on the 2nd of July 1860. He subsequently married a daughter of Thomas Gilham, Maria, on the 7th of July 1874. She had also been widowed and was Maria Taylor when he married her. Her first husband, John Taylor, had died just months previously on the 3rd of September 1873, when he had a seizure whilst smoking in bed and setting fire to his bedding! They had had a daughter, Emily Maria, in 1877. After Williams death in 1885, Maria married for a third time - a Laurence Burns - whom she outlived by two years.

John senior and Catherine lived at Tea Tree Farm, near Bagdad, where he was a farmer. On Wednesday the 30th of January 1856, Catherine was driving her mare home from market, as she did every alternate week. What happened next is best described by the Colonial Times from Hobart on Saturday the 2nd of February 1856.

Taken from the Colonial Times, Hobart, Saturday 2nd February 1856 page 3.

THE FATAL ACCIDENT AT O'BRIEN'S BRIDGE - INQUEST ON MRS BAILEY.

Yesterday an inquest was held at the house of Mr. Stevenson, Dusty Miller, O'Brien's Bridge before A. B. Jones Esq., coroner, on view of the body of Catherine Bailey, who died on Wednesday from injuries sustained by falling from a cart on the afternoon of that day.

The following jury was sworn: Messrs. James Hickson, (foreman) English Corney, W. Stevenson, Henry

Carpenter, Thomas Smith, John Walduck, and Thomas Archer.

The coroner stated that the death they had to enquire into, was that of the wife of a farmer residing at the "Tea Tree," (Tea Tree Farm) near Bagdad, who was returning home on the afternoon of Wednesday last, and was thrown out of the vehicle in which she was riding, and brought into that house almost in a state of insensibility, and died in a few hours afterwards. It so happened that Dr. Keen was near the spot and saw her. It was stated that she was thrown out by some person in another cart running against her, and if such were the case, it might occasion serious consequences on the party, and great caution would be required to be exercised by the jury. It was his (the coroner's) duty to state the facts as they had been stated to him, and it was for the jury to give what attention was necessary. He had been informed that the deceased was on the wrong side of the road, and was in a state of intoxication. If that were the case, it would relieve the party in a great measure from blame. A person might be on the wrong side, and a person going along might see them, he should himself (and he was an old whip) expect that the person would move out of the way ; but if the person were intoxicated, he would keep on, and there would be a collision. If, as was stated, the vehicle on this occasion were run into, and the party who did it took no notice of what occurred, they would all blame him for want of feeling but the question was whether he had done any act of which the law could take cognizance. If the deceased was intoxicated, and on her wrong side, then it would be her own fault. It was not known who the party was. There was a party who stated that he saw someone going along in a cart, and that party had been summoned, but at the present moment they were in the dark who the party was; they did not know who had done the act. It was necessary deceased should be opened, for there were no marks of violence on deceased's body, and there were no means by which the medical witness could positively state the cause of death, as she might have had something given her, or she might have died of apoplexy. The coroner had, therefore (although it might not have been agreeable to *the wishes of the relatives), been obliged to authorise the doctor to open the body.*

The coroner, jury, and witnesses then proceeded to view the body, which was in a room of the inn. On their return to the inquest room the following evidence was taken:-

John Bailey, a farmer residing at the Tea Tree, near Bagdad, husband of deceased, deposed that, he last saw deceased alive on Wednesday morning, when she left home with a horse and chaise cart, to bring the produce of the farm to town, as she had been in the habit of doing for the last six years once a fortnight, She was in her usual state of good health, and in her right senses. He never knew her to be in any other. He never saw her again till he saw her lying dead at the Dusty Miller, on Thursday morning. She was never in the habit of drinking to excess when from home. She had been his wife for seven and forty years. She was fifty-nine years of age. (She was actually sixty three and they had been married forty-four years, not as stated which would have made her twelve at the time of their marriage and he thirteen!) *James Fitzgerald, a ticket-of-leave man,* ostler at Mr. Mason's, the Traveller's Rest, Glenorchy, deposed that he knew deceased by sight, On Wednesday last, about two in the afternoon, witness was going to town from Mr. Mason's, with a cart of his master's. When he came near Mr. Brewer's, on the O'Brien's Bridge Road, he met a mare that he knew to be Mrs. Bailey's trotting along the road towards him, with reins round her leg, and the harness broken. Witness caught her and tied her up, and went on towards town. He had not got a quarter of a mile, when he saw Mrs. Bailey's chaise cart standing at the side of the road, with the shafts on the bank at the left hand side as you go into town. Mrs. Bailey was lying near the cart. One of the shafts, the right, had been driven into the bank. ripping the bank nine or ten inches. Witness saw Dr. Keen and one of Rev. Mr. Bennett's men, four or five yards off. Dr. Keen assisted me to put her into the cart. She fainted as soon as they put her in, when they took her out again, witness went on to town.

Witness observed tracks of two carts on the right hand side, as if they had come together, and had been *dragged across the road to where the cart was standing. He had seen another chaise cart going on towards Hobart Town before he saw Mrs Bailey's horse. It passed him on the road, the same way that he was going. It was driven by a man, who was the only person in the cart. He was drunk, and witness thought he would have fallen out of the cart as he passed. In the cart were some baskets and a box but he could not say what were in the baskets. Witness thought he would know the cart again; it was a bay horse with a white star on the forehead. Did not see any writing on the cart. Witness would know the man again: he was a man of middling height, rather dark coloured, in his shirt sleeves, black waistcoat. and a dark cloth cap. Witness was forced to keep as close to the bank as he could when the man passed. Witness did not think he knew where he was going. When witness got in sight of Mrs. Bailey's cart he saw the other man going on as fast as it could in the centre of the road, witness being on the top of the hill, by Mr. Read's, at that time. No other vehicle was in sight then. Witness did not observe that any part of Mrs. Bailey's cart was broken, but he saw a mark of a graze on the off shaft,* near the point, which looked as if it was newly done, and as if something had come in contact with it. Witness had been about nine months at Mr. Mason's, the Traveller's Rest. Mr. Armstrong supplied Mr. Mason with ginger beer. Did not see Mr. Armstrong's cart that day, nor Mr. Emmett's cart. Mr. Emmett's cart was up the road on Tuesday. Mrs. Bailey said, in witness's hearing, her side pained her, and she was unable to sit up. Witness could not say whether she was sober or not.

By the Jury - Mrs. Bailey told me a chaise cart, which had just passed had run into her.

Dr. Keen deposed, that he saw deceased about one o'clock on Wednesday, lying on her back in the road, and saw the cart five hundred yards off. Witness examined her, saw a bruise on her right temple. On attempting to raise her, witness found she was faint, and after some unavoidable delay, she was removed to the Dusty Miller, where he remained with her four hours and a half. She said she had had two glasses of beer; witness had no reason to think she had had more. Syncope was her chief symptom. Witness saw her again at eleven the same

126

night, when he found she had died at nine o'clock. The witness described the result of the post mortem examination, the principal injury being in the region of the spleen. A heavy fall of such a person as deceased, who was stout and fat, would produce the effects he observed, and which she could not have survived. Deceased made one or two incoherent statements to describe how the accident occurred, calling on "that vagabond" who had run into her, and asking witness to go after him and find out who he was. Witness also gleaned from her that she had followed her horse so far, and had fallen down four or five hundred yards from the cart, not being able to go any further. The witness (in reply to the coroner) said, the harness was broken, it was very rotten, and he wondered it could have drawn the cart which was heavily laden. A little girl about four or five years old was in the cart, crying very much: she was deceased's grand-daughter. The injury to the spleen was mortal, and fully accounted for the constant symptoms of syncope she exhibited.

Witness did not observe any marks on the road, he did not look for any. It appeared to him as if the cart had fallen down, and the harness broken, and deceased's fall would have been quite enough to produce injury.

The jury here proceeded to the yard of the Dusty Miller to inspect the harness, cart, &c, when the harness and backbands appeared to be of so ancient and rotten a character, that the jury expressed surprise that it could have carried even the cart much less a loaded one. There were no marks on the cart of anything having come in collision with it. Mr. D C Thomas gave evidence to this point, and as to the contents of the cart at the time of the accident, namely, a bag of sugar, part of a bag of flour, three boxes, &c.

Mrs. Stevenson, the landlady of the Dusty Miller, deposed to having been present at the death of Mrs. Bailey, which took place at nine o clock on Wednesday night. Deceased was quite sensible shortly before, and told witness a cart had run against her, and thrown her out. She appeared to be quite sober. She was not aware she was dying.

The court was cleared, and the jury deliberated for some time, but could not agree to a verdict, without the evidence of Mr. Cooley's driver, who was stated to have met the deceased on Wednesday at New Town, and who could depose to her state on that occasion.

The coroner therefore adjourned the enquiry to Tuesday next, at two o'clock

Note: A verdict of Accidental Death was given at the inquest on this later date, 5th February 1856. O'Brien's Bridge is now called Glenorchy.

So John had lost his Catherine. The whole family were shocked and devastated. George felt suddenly old and somewhat frail. First Richard and then he had heard of the deaths of William Wire and Sarah Pierce; now poor Catherine. All of the old crowd were going. They were all getting old. George felt tired. He wasn't up to much. His body ached most days and for some time he had suffered a pain in his right upper abdomen. It started as a discomfort, but lately it had hurt. It quite put him off eating. He sighed as he and Bet left John with his children to mourn in private. Bet was getting old too! She had put up with much during their marriage, yes that much was true, but both had enjoyed a good life and some great times too. At least life hadn't been dull for them.

George and Bet lived out their lives quietly in their later years. He could not afford the rents on lands he could not work and so they settled without too much ceremony in their modest wooden house in the Falls area of New Norfolk, and watched their grandchildren grow. Every day George felt frailer and moved more slowly. His pain increased in his side and he lost his once healthy appetite. His skin took on a yellowish hue and he lost weight. Did he have liver or pancreatic cancer possibly? Finally on Saturday the 25th of October 1856 he passed away peacefully at home. The cause of death was listed as 'jaundice'. Bet was devastated. His friend and neighbour George Nesbit registered his death as Bet felt too frail and grief stricken to manage it. **The Hobart Courier for Monday 27th October 1856** read as follows-

DEATH

At the Falls, New Norfolk on Saturday 25th instant, GEORGE RANSLEY, aged 78, leaving a large family to deplore his loss, and respected by all who knew him. His funeral will take place *on Wednesday next at 2 o'clock. Friends will please to accept this as an invitation.*

Bet lived on until Thursday the 30th of December 1858 when she died, at home, from 'natural causes'. They are both buried in the church of St John the Evangelist at Plenty. It is as small a church, and in as peaceful a spot, as St Rumwold's where they were united almost fifty years previously!

Into the Future

The future belongs to those who believe in the beauty of their dreams. (Eleanor Roosevelt)

It felt like the end, but it was just the beginning. The beginning of a dynasty - a wonderful nation - in which each person played their part to make Van Diemen's Land the country we know today.

It was in 1856, the year that Catherine Bailey and George Ransley died, that the name of the colony was changed to Tasmania. A new world, a new generation and, shortly, no more convicts would be sent there; its peoples would all be free. In fact Tasmania received no further convict consignments after 1853 and Australia followed suit in 1868. The people would be able to build an exciting new land amongst the natural beauty and unique creatures that make up that part of the world.

The older generation started to pass away – Rhoda Pool, as she was then, died on the October of 24th 1862 at her home in Oatlands from bronchitis. She was sixty six years old and listed as the 'wife of a farmer'. Her husband, John Pool, registered her death. They had sixteen years of married life together. John Pool died in Ulverstone on the 26th of October 1887 from 'senile decay' he was eighty eight.

Samuel Bailey died just a week or so before his younger uncle, John. Samuel died on the 27th of January 1866 at Oatlands, where he had lived not far from his sister, Rhoda. His cause of death was listed as 'old age and infirmity'. He was eighty and listed as a farmer. He is buried at Oatlands Methodist cemetery.

John, his uncle, died on the 8th of February 1866 aged seventy three in New Norfolk of 'decay of nature'. He was also listed as a farmer and his death was registered by William Williams, his grandson, son of John's daughter Elizabeth and her husband Robert Williams.

John Bailey junior had married Fanny Remy Kenny, who was some eleven years younger than himself, in 1856. They had baby Sarah Jane in the same year, followed by Elizabeth in 1862, Samuel Pantry Bailey in 1866 and Fanny Kenny Bailey in 1870. Thus the name of 'Pantry' was once more associated with the Bailey's!

In 1863 there was a double wedding at St John the Evangelist, River Plenty in New Norfolk, when Matilda and Charles Fenton's son, Henry Fenton. married his cousin

Marianne Ransley, in a double wedding with John Ransley's grandson Robert and his cousin Rachel Fenton. They married on the 23rd of April and among the witnesses were John's daughter, Amelia, and her uncle James Henry Salter.

Matilda was the first of George and Bet's children to die. In the days before anti-biotics, little could be done to help with infection. In 1868, aged sixty, Mattie had a bad chest infection and died on the 13th of June from congestion of the lungs. Anne died in 1874 aged fifty six. By then she and her husband, William Gundry, were living in Victoria and that was where she died. Edward followed in 1877, from pneumonia, in Hobart. He was fifty five years old. James died in Hamilton from consumption aged fifty eight on the 17th of May 1881. On the 17th of February 1882 John died in New Norfolk aged seventy, from septicaemia caused by Erysipilus. He is also buried in St John the Evangelist churchyard at Plenty. Robert also succumbed to pneumonia, but was aged seventy four. He died on the 16th of June 1896 in Ellendale. He had survived his wife Margaret by just three days. George junior died in New Norfolk on the 3rd of December 1904, and Hannah died in 1908, also in New Norfolk.

John Ransley and his wife Mary – née Salter - had fourteen surviving children, ten daughters and four sons. One of these, John, born on the 13th of February 1852 married Mary Ann Godfrey, who was a domestic residing at her father's house in Brighton. She was born on the 8th of February 1857. They married in Fenton Forest on the 6th of February 1875 when he was twenty two and she was eighteen. They had several children - five daughters and six sons. John was born in 1879, Samuel Gilbert in 1881, George William in 1882, Charles William in 1883, Alexander Banks in 1886. All of these children were born in Fentonbury, Hamilton.

In 1894 Mary was pregnant again. After a short, but painful, labour Albert was born on the 17th of September. When the women had bathed Mary and swaddled the baby, John went into the room to meet his new son. Mary was sitting up in bed, her face was red and shiny and her damp greying brown hair clung to her forehead. In her arms she held the baby. His perfect little thumb was in his mouth and his eyes were closed tight against the ray of bright sunlight that streamed in through a chink in the curtain. Mary smiled as she handed him to John. "Meet Albert, your new son!" she exclaimed with a weak smile. John Ransley looked down on Albert, the small perfect being in his arms. "Hello little nipper!" he said, and felt the familiar surge of love he had always felt when he gazed upon his future!

All the members of the gang - Ransleys, Baileys, Higgins, Hogbens, Questeds, Giles, Gilhams, Pierces and Denards, plus of course, Smeed and Wires - played their part in the founding of the nation and its people that we know today as Tasmania. Leaving all they knew to take a journey of several months to the other side of the world took courage. The women too were courageous. They had given up their homes and left their friends and their parents forever. The men, of course, had no choice in the matter. They had spent their time on the hulks and then endured the seemingly endless journey on the *Governor Ready* - with all of the hardships and perils that that entailed. All of this had taken stamina and resilience. To then be put to work for strangers in an unknown land (in an alien landscape with all the new dangers that that would have involved) may well have made a short swing at the end of a hempen rope on Penenden Heath seem like the easy option!

Unsurprisingly, they all made a success of their lives in the colony. The very qualities that had made them successful free traders in Kent - courage, audacity, endurance and imagination – all those qualities that the British Government viewed with disgust and contempt! Those were the qualities needed to, not only survive, but to thrive and make a successful new world in which their children, grandchildren and many great grandchildren could safely grow up.

Tasmanians today have those same brave qualities. The land is like nowhere else on Earth. It seems to have its own eco –system, its own unique landscape and creatures that are found nowhere else on the planet; but yet, it is homely. A Brit feels very easy there and the British way of life is understood and compatible with the place. This fact is undoubtedly down to those early settlers - the pioneers and exiles from their homeland who made the country we can see today. This is a country I have come to love and feel at home in. Those convicts were cast out and banished from the land of their birth to a little known, and sometimes hostile, country to make a new life and build a nation. I, for one, am so thankful that they did.

Embrace the change, no matter what it is; once you do, you can learn about the new world you're in and take advantage of it

Nikki Giovanni

Epilogue

When I finished 'Gentlemen in Blue', I felt that it was the end of an era, but the beginning of a new journey. I had thoroughly enjoyed the research, and I really felt that I knew George Ransley and the other gang members as if they had been close friends. Through social media I had, miraculously, (and very easily, I might add) found some Ransleys in Tasmania. It was they, and our mutual close friend, Tony Hale, who suggested that I write a sequel about the lives of the gang after their arrival in Tasmania.

I started off not really knowing what I was going to discover; however, there is a wealth of information waiting to be found. Truly the internet is a wonderful place and my research was fascinating.

There are a great many descendants of most of the gang member's still living in Tasmania and on mainland Australia. Of course, there are many still living in Kent. Kentish folk have long memories and, in the Walnut Tree Inn, Aldington, George and the gang are still very much alive to the locals. I would love to see a reunion there one day of all of the gang's descendants! What a lot of toasts would be drunk to the Aldington blues! I know that the gang would feel completely at home there as little has changed since they quaffed their tankards of ale and their feet wore down the old brick step running along the bar!

I had the inestimable pleasure of visiting Tasmania in November 2018. I had tracked down various descendants of some of the gang members through social media and, here in Kent, England, through readers of my works. I have met with descendants of Cephas and James Quested, John Bailey and Thomas Gilham. I know a descendant of James Hogben - we had been friends for twenty years before we realised the link. I have met with several Ransleys, some of whom consider me to be honorary family! One of John and Mary Ann Godfrey's sons, Samuel Gilbert, is the grandfather of Mr Dennis Ransley - who kindly entertained me at an excellent luncheon in Hobart Tasmania during my 2018 visit (along with Mr Stephen Figg and Mr Van Ransley) - all descendants of George's children. I have become very good friends with the Grandsons of Albert, John and Mary's youngest son, and the baby, born at the end of my story. All of these are great-great-great grandsons of George Ransley and his wife Elizabeth. They are Paul, Bruce, and Mark. Megan, their cousin, and her brother David (plus their cousins Kit and Tim, who I have not yet met) are all descended from Albert and, therefore, George. I am proud to call them my friends, and I shall be returning to Tasmania very soon by the kind invitation of Mr Mark Ransley.

Our boys and their families would have felt very much at home in the New Norfolk, Upper Derwent and Derwent Valley areas. They are quite like Kent in landscape and not dissimilar in climate. There have been hop fields in New Norfolk since 1846, like the Kentish ones. Indeed our Kentish lads would have known a thing or two about hop grafting and growing since Kent was a huge hop growing county. The Bush Inn in New Norfolk is like many a Georgian hostelry in Kent, and has a wealth of antique artefacts inside it. I have always felt the spirit of the Aldington Blues as I traverse the Romney Marshes and the villages around Aldington, Bonnington and Bilsington. Amazingly, I felt that also when I visited New Norfolk and the river Derwent; and, as I stood in the little churchyard of St John the Evangelist at Plenty with Ransley descendants, it was very moving for us all. Yes, I am sure their spirits live on but, better still, so do their descendants. They encapsulate the tenacity, resourcefulness and greatness of their ancestors and I am so grateful to have met them.

Owler's Moon

On Romney Marsh you may feel a little closer to your God
But tread the secret marsh paths where smuggling men have trod.
By the Dymchurch wall and down among the reeds
Went the busy Owlers, about their silent deeds.

Wading through the shallows with fine French lace and brandy,
Always mindful where to tread, but with a pistol handy;
Lest Excisemen might set a trap by misty dyke or dune,
And spoil a perfect smuggling night-lit by an Owler's moon.

The ponies head for Aldington where Captain Batts did stand,
Waiting for his gang of Blues, with shrouded lamp in hand.
With luck his owlers will be home and drinking rum-laced tea
Long before the excise cutter can safe put out to sea.

But whilst you imagine all these larks, let me give you a warning —
There's one bad lot you don't want to meet on a dark blown
morning.
Steer clear of the Hawkhurst gang, they don't take kind to a
stranger,
And they'll tend to shoot you where you stand, so you won't be a
danger.
When they're leading up their ponies carrying the casks,
And up to no little mischief with their smuggling tasks.

Now there's musket shots by Brookland church in the misty night,

Sounds like a gang of Owlers are in a running fight –

And 'mid sword-slash curse and musket ball

Grave wounded see an Owler fall;

His smuggling days now I fear are over

They'll drag him off to Maidst'n or Dover'

Where he'll like stand trial for his crimes;

On Romney Marsh these are desperate times.

And at Penenden stands a gibbet on that godless heath alone

Where carrion birds pick off the flesh from many a smuggler's bone.

Trevor Harrison July 2000

Bibliography

Libraries of Tasmania - Linc (on-line archives of Tasmania)

The wicked Trade – John Douch

The Smugglers – (Vol 11) Lord Teignmouth and Charles G Harper

Lynne's Family – Lynne's Tasmanian family on-line

The Assignment System of Convict labour in VDL – 1824 - 1842

Thesis 1959- Anne McKay

Founders and Survivors (on line)

Trove Newspaper archives on-line (for the Colonial Times and the Hobart Courier)

Surgeons Journal from *HMS Harmony* 1827 – Mr William Clifford, Ships Surgeon Superintendent

Convict Records of Australia

Gentlemen in Blue – Lyn Watts

Convict Indents (ship and arrival registers, ships musters) 1788 - 1868

The Convict Ships 1787 – 1868 – Charles Bateson

Family History (for Thomas Gilham) – Sue Rodaughan

Ancestry.co.uk

International Genealogical Index (IGI)

Smuggling in Kent and Sussex 1700 – 1840 – Mary Waugh

Kent Country Churches – James Anthony Syms

The National Library of Australia – Convict Assignment

Convicts to Australia – research guide on-line- Life on a convict ship

Digital Panopticon – arriving in Australia

Also available by the same author

- **Traders of the Fifth Continent – Tales of Smugglers and Rascals on the Romney Marsh (March 2015)**
- **The Dark Lantern (and other Tales)**
  A collection of short stories (July 2016)
- **Gentlemen in Blue – the story of George Ransley and the Aldington Gang (January 2018)**
- **Sister at the Sharp End – Nursing Experiences from the 1970s and 1980s (August 2018)**

- **Enter at A and other Tales of Terror – handy tips for the Dressage Rookie (November 2018)**
- **Coffee Time Killer**
  A collection of short stories (March 2019)

These are available from WattKnott Publishing
Testers, Whatlington, Battle, East Sussex TN33 0NS
Or email: lyncharliewatts@hotmail.co.uk

All are also available from Ebay or Amazon

➢ All can be found on Kindle except for 'Enter at A'